VOICES OF UKRAINE

Impressions Around a War

EDITED BY LEAH BLOCK

A PUBLICATION OF THE INTERNATIONAL HUMAN RIGHTS
ART FESTIVAL (IHRAF)

VOICES OF UKRAINE:
IMPRESSIONS AROUND A WAR

First printing edition 2022

Printed by IHRAF in the United States of America.
IHRAF, New York City, USA
https://www.ihraf.org/

Design by Michele Chu
Cover photo by Kostiantyn Stupak/Unsplash

CONTENTS

INTRODUCTION

It is with both sadness and hope that the *International Human Rights Art Festival* publishes this volume of Ukrainian writers and artists, living both inside and outside of that beleaguered country.

Although war is ubiquitous within human history—authors Will and Ariel Durant, writing in The Story of Civilization, assured that there have been only 268 scattered years without war over the past 3,400+ years of human history—war's annihilative and barbaric energy never ceases to horrify us anew.

Though wars are initiated by single leaders, from the Assyrian Sennacherib (d. 681 BCE) to Vladimir Putin (currently alive), it is thousands of foot soldiers who do the actual damage. How, we ask ourselves, can there be so many fellow humans willing to abandon all personal morality and obliterate cities, civilians and children? What does this say about us?

On the other hand are the poets, the philosophers, the artists, the peacemakers—those who exhibit the highest qualities of human nature. Sometimes victims of this grotesque political game, sometimes observers, it is they who most bring compassion to a world gone mad.

In this folio, we gather together voices under siege, to show how even in the most horrifying of times, beauty, sincerity and emotional vulnerability can point the way toward a deeper connection with ourselves, and with each other. In the face of this vile onslaught, these Ukrainian writers have opened their hearts and souls to us. They bring the highest form of human creativity to us: the sublime. The combination of a vulnerable pain, and beauty.

It is with appreciation, humility and deep respect that we publish this anthology.

Tom Block
Executive Director,
International Human Rights Art Festival
New York City
April 2022

I WOULD LIKE TO KEEP

Maria Dziedzan

I would like to keep…
the shrine at the crossroads which my father paid to restore; the lane to the village flanked by fields of sunflowers, bordered by the froth of chest-high dill and lined by cherry trees, not planted for their fruit or their beauty but to show where the road is in Winter snows.

I would like to walk up…
the drive beside the rose garden with its overblown blooms lying heavy in the sunshine and to sit on the bench in the shade of the walnut tree while my cousin, Halia, breaks open a jar of birch sap which she collected at the first call of Spring. I would like to see her set the jar back on the shelves of her larder filled with jewelled fruits for the Winter.

I would like to see her…
feeding her poultry, the turkey fooled by ducks' and hens' eggs into rearing a multicultural brood of chicks. "Turkeys make the best mothers," she tells me. Her daughter gathers strawberries from her pocket-money garden, to treat us to dessert at tea-time.

I would like to step across...
the gaggle of shoes at the door to the house as the four generations who live here try to keep Summer's dust outside, and perch on a stool at the table which is never big enough, while the littlest boy climbs onto my knee. Not because he loves me, but because the guest gets the best first.

I would like to see...
the ebb and flow of the household all crammed into one large kitchen, while the rooms of state sit silent and empty. The guests, and then the children, are fed with the scraps thrown straight into the bucket for the pig. The cow lumbers home from pasture and my cousin's work moves from the kitchen to the barn and back to the kitchen to feed the men in from the fields. The timbre of voices changes and the men tease the small boys and wait to be fed before putting the world to rights.

I would like to see...
the dusk come creeping up from the valley dragging its accomplice, the river mist, with it. A pre-slumberous quiet falls and, replete with fresh air, we take to our beds while my cousin kneels at her little shrine in the shadows under the stairs, hands clasped, to pray for her brood in a whisper which only God is meant to hear.

BUTTERFLIES

Olga Nadukhovskaya

YELLOW-BLUE SKY

Sofiia Krazhan

Click click click.

The typing on my keyboard gets louder as the darker hours of the night begin to creep in. The lounge of Lipton Hall, NYU is either filling up or thinning, I cannot tell. I am staring at a screen trying to finally finish a stupid 300 word paper about Thomas Hobbes and his contributions to our understanding of political theory. Outraged at him for writing some old text about authoritarian society and claiming he cares about liberty. Speaking as if the two are in some way intertwined. My mind is numbing the more I stare at the screen.

The glass walls of the room I am in allow me to see the other students talking, drinking vending machine-supplied Powerade, and munching on stale chips they brought back from their dorms. Some of them are working. Some of them have their computers open and have highlighters in their hands. The chatter of the people next to me is not a good white noise. Their conversation is funny. One of them makes a joke about the way my friend says the word "thanks." He says that if we were to ever get kidnapped, she would annoy the kidnappers so much that they would drop her off back at her dorm in half an hour and she would say "Thanks," the same way she would if she was accepting a Cola.

Buzz buzz buzz.

Expecting a text from my partner, I lift my phone from the table. My notifications are silenced. My message preview is off. All I can see is my mom's contact title, her photo, and the number of texts rapidly increasing. 1, 2, 3, 4, 5. I didn't think too much of it at first. Until I realize that 22:30 for me is 5:30 for my mother. She should not be awake yet.

My mother always tends to start every one of our text conversations with an ominous, singular word: my name. She follows it with "Hi" or a question, a text about how I am doing or reminding me to check if I am completing my tasks on time. I am obliged often to reply immediately because if not, she freaks out.

I open the WhatsApp conversation, and my heart starts beating so fast that I think it stops.

"В Україні війна" There's war in Ukraine.

"Росіяни напали" The Russians attacked.

"Бережи себе" Protect yourself.

My fingers begin to tremble. I can barely keep my hands still as my eyes well up with tears. *Not again* are the only words that come to mind. My lungs can barely take in enough oxygen as my mind is suddenly torn to shreds. Where are my cousins, where are my aunts and where are my uncles? They all live in Kyiv. Almost as if she read my mind, another buzz.

"Київ бомбять" They're bombing Kyiv.

Every cell in my body begins to shake with fear. My home city. The place I was born, took my first steps, said my first words, is under fire. I begin to cry—in the study lounge of my dorm building. A pit feeling sinks inside and I am at a loss. I do not understand, what did we do? I follow Ukrainian politics as closely as I can, and there was no incitation of violence towards Russia. Nothing should have provoked this attack. And yet before I could stop myself, my inner child jumps out.

Where is my dad?

He was renovating the apartment from back home. The apartment my parents were to retire in, the apartment in which my grandmother was visiting just weeks earlier. My heart begins to beat so fast that I cannot keep my ribcage still. I start to breathe louder, tears running down my cheeks as I stare at the people near me. They all begin to ask what is wrong with me, but I cannot find the words. My father is in danger. I could lose my father.

Bang bang bang.

A residential tower was hit in Kyiv. Floors were destroyed, and people screamed at 5 o'clock on a Thursday morning. Twenty-four hours before, those citizens were enjoying a warm cup of tea with honey cakes, maybe eating borsh, a natively Ukrainian dish, appropriated by Russia long enough ago that they made it their national dish, possibly reading a newspaper about how Ukrainians are coming together in peace and unity. Now their home is destroyed. In the apartment into which they invested their money, time, and effort, their life is now blown to bits. For nothing.

My extended family's locations, as well as my father's, turn off. I cannot see them on the map through Apple's system. They do not know how to turn off their locations, which means that they lost their phone service. They're underground. Hiding in bomb shelters, trying to find hope in a situation that seems to be nothing but "shocking" to the rest of the world.

Everyone watches in disbelief. But why are they watching?

All they do is stand by, while forty million people are crying, children are screaming for their mothers and fathers, boys who barely turned 18 are forced to fight a war they did not ask for, women cannot bring their children into the world without fear that both of them will be able to make it through the night.

Boom boom boom.

On the streets of Chernihiv, innocent civilians are shot down when they're waiting in line for groceries. The last of what's left. Мрія ("Dream") is destroyed. The road signs are torn down for the Russians to not get to Kyiv. Refugees flood the border. Mariupol's maternity wards are destroyed, theaters are crushed into the ground, people cry as they attempt to save themselves from bullets. Irpin is now a mass graveyard, rather than a suburban town that prospered.

Quiet nights are now a blessing. The earth for which my great grandfather fought is now covered in my brethren's blood. The Kremlin threatened to place Ukrainians into camps. The same camps that not even 100 years ago, Ukrainians had to be liberated from.

Liberated from what? From whom? The freedom of the fall of the Soviet Union? The joy of independence and the nation's pride?

Pop pop pop.

I send my grandmother a text. It sends it to the system, but it has not been delivered to her. She is lost. My grandfather, whose body is ridden with cancer, cannot get medicine that ships into pharmacies, because they are barricaded by the troops. "The liberators" they call themselves.

Two hundred thousand Russians stood in celebration of Crimea's annexation in Moscow, in the Red Square in 2014. A part of our history that Ukrainians mourn. We cry for our Crimean brothers and sisters who are under siege from the political power whose greed seems insatiable.

Five thousand Russians came out to rally against the war. Only one had the strength to stand up against propaganda on local news. A single ballerina from the Bolshoi Theatre left the country to dance for the Netherlands.

Do not infantilize the adults that support the man you blame daily.

Ivan Kuliak, a Russian gymnast, barely 21, landing third in the Olympics, wore a pro-war symbol on his chest as he stood on the panel. His joke of an excuse was that he felt the Ukrainians were rude when we shout "Слава Україні! (Glory to Ukraine)," a national salute that has existed since 1917.

Kuliak stood third next to the champion in Doha. A man who wore the blue and yellow colors of the sky and sunflowers of my home. A man whose native tongue was as Ukrainian as mine, one who surpassed all the challenges to make it to first. In the midst of war.

I cried in my dorm when I saw my mother's face. She could barely keep her voice still as she stared at me on FaceTime. I was the one secure person in her life left. Her eyes reddened as she told me the building I grew up in no longer exists. She held a napkin to her face and sobbed.

I had never seen my mother cry.

And I will never go through that heartbreak again. Because as long as the sun rises and sets, as long as the sunflowers bloom in our fields and our people fight back, Ukraine will stand. Against anyone who comes its way. Our blood was spilled once before and we came out victorious. And we will do so again. Because Україна понад усе.

Ще не вмерла України, ні слава, ні воля,
Ще нам, браття молодії, усміхнеться доля!
Згинуть наші воріженьки, як роса на сонці,
Запануєм і ми, браття, у своїй сторонці!
Душу й тіло ми положим за нашу свободу
І—покажем, що ми, браття, козацького роду!
Душу й тіло ми положим за нашу свободу
І—покажем, що ми, браття, козацького роду!

Ukraine is not dead yet, neither glory nor freedom,
Fate will smile on us, young brothers!
Our enemies will perish like dew in the sun,
Let us rule, brothers, in our side!
We will lay down our souls and bodies for our freedom
And—let's show that we, brothers, of the Cossack family!
We will lay down our souls and bodies for our freedom
And—let's show that we, brothers, of the Cossack family!

WAR IN UKRAINE

Olena Prygoda

VANYA

Tatyana Shramko

GHOSTS OF MARIUPOL

Nick Herring

My family left Ukraine on my daughter's 4th birthday. She doesn't know the word 'war'. She thinks that explosions are salutes. Because I told her so.

I said 'Goodbye' to her then. And it sounded... thundering.

The words 'good night' and 'take care' and even 'see you soon' sound different now. Have more weight to them. And you always mean it.

Initially, I wanted to write a story about myself in the time of war. But then I thought it would be selfish. I am not the character deserving attention.

Mariupol is.

For you, 'Mariupol' is the name of a Ukrainian city famous only for its diabolical misfortune, plaguing world headlines in March 2022. But for Ukrainians, this one word is a heavy and complex message.

Now, this may be uncomfortable to read, but I will suggest no reader's discretion. Comfortable or not, everyone must suffer through it to learn the truth.

Imagine your city. Your street, your house, the people living there, walking their dogs, dating, strolling. Living their lives. And now imagine it all gone. And not just 'poof', as in vaporized into thin air. Imagine it replaced by Hell.

The city is littered with the dead and parts of the dead.

There was a boy with half his face missing.

There was a girl with no legs.

There was another girl trying to wake up a mother who wouldn't wake up.

All the things that your mind subconsciously seals away to the corners of your corneas, are there. Right now. As real as you and me.

You may strain your imagination to exhaustion, but there is nothing you can picture that will be horrible enough to match what is happening right now in a city not that far from you (if you are a European dweller).

Those who have survived Mariupol are probably not afraid of going to Hell anymore. I mean, how much worse can it get?

No one collects the dead. For the first four or five days, Mariupol's locals tried to get the bodies off the streets and give proper burials (which is basically a pit of corpses with a volunteer reading a prayer), then stopped, as the shelling would simply kill you as well, and somebody would have to pick your corpse now. So they just lie there. In the streets, on the very spots they died. Just feast for the crows. Rotting. Decomposing at their own pace. With sunken cheeks. Hollow faces. Eyeless. And this is not some *Game of Thrones* scenery. This is not an author's imagination. This is the center of Europe in 2022.

Since the Dark Ages, there has been an unwritten rule to ceasefire in order to collect the dead. No such rules are known to the Russians. They continue shelling 24/7, as if to say, 'Don't you even lift your head up'. How far have they fallen?

Imagine people—adults, children, the elderly, the sick, the healthy, the strong, the weak; pregnant, asthmatic, someone whose birthday is today, someone who got married a month ago, someone nursing a baby—all cowering in a basement so filled with people that you can barely breathe.

And this torture just goes on and on.

The Russians cut off Mariupol from the outside completely.

No one comes in. No one comes out.

There is nothing to eat.

There is nothing to drink.

There is nothing to treat yourself with.

You don't see the sun.

If you want to tell your relatives in another city that you are alright, you can write it on a piece of paper and hope that one day it will be found on your corpse. Because no digital connection works in the city. The radio towers were the first things the Russians brought down.

They deliberately allow no food inside. One woman was miraculously saved when she was about to kill her dog to cook it for her family and herself.

They deliberately took the water supply out. In the beginning of March, snow fell in Mariupol. So people melted that snow to take a sip in turns.

All the pharmacies were leveled in the first days, as if targeted on purpose. If you have asthma or diabetes, or a heart condition, then you just lost the Russian roulette.

You don't come out of the bomb shelter, as the shelling just never stops.

If you have a cat or a dog, imagine putting it in a cage. You cover the cage with a blanket so that only a fraction of light comes inside. And then you keep it there. For three weeks. With no food. With water barely enough to continue breathing. Meanwhile, you take a metal rod. Each day for 15 hours you occasionally hammer the cage with this rod. And you never look inside. You don't let it know what will happen next. You never talk to the creature. You don't let it know whether you care or not. You never even listen to its squeals, or cries, or wails, or whatever it is at that point.

I am in Kyiv. We have food in the stores. Not as abundant as in times of peace, but a decent menu nonetheless. A little more expensive than usual, but affordable. And every time I put food on my plate, I think of those who can't. Every time I sip my tea, I think of the people who would kill for a gulp. Every time I go outside, I think of the people who live underground.

This is Mariupol.
Welcome.

In one month of the siege of Mariupol, Russians destroyed 2,340 apartment blocks and 61,000 private houses and buildings. As if trying to say, 'You have nowhere to go; nowhere is safe'.

7 hospitals and 3 clinics—those they aimed at most precisely. As if trying to maximize the hate.

7 institutes. 57 schools. 70 kindergartens. 3 birth houses. Because fighting the pregnant and kids is safer than fighting the Ukrainian resistance.

9 out of 10 buildings have at least one wall missing. There are probably no windows in the whole city that are in one piece.

The only thing that remains intact are the freshly dug graveyards that are practically in every yard now.

Each of the destroyed buildings is a small loss. We'll rebuild houses, raise hospitals, put up schools. Every brick of every house we'll make anew. We are good at that. We are good at healing our country. Had a lot of historical chances to practice.

But there are things which cannot be mended.

The number of estimated dead in Mariupol is changing constantly. Among the dead are more than a hundred children. More than a hundred little humans with tender voices and plans for the summer. Even one such life is worth ending the war for. Mind you, these are only the confirmed deaths, not including the unaccounted for or the missing. Some of the latter are technically alive, but buried underneath the concrete rubble. And 'buried alive' is not a figure of speech anymore.

After a month of the war, 170,000 people were still in Mariupol. Besieged. Starved. Surviving on dog food. Hunting pigeons. Unable to speak because of thirst. Unable to walk. Unable to think. Can you even call that 'alive'? The city covered them with its mutilated and crippled body, trying to preserve the most precious—the people, the soul of the city.

To think that once, Mariupol homed almost half a million.

Ukrainians are satirical folk. Often enough we use humor as a way of fighting fear. We joke about Chornobaivka, Putin, Kadyrov, NATO, Biden, the EU, Zelensky... you name it. We joke about bombing and artillery, and rockets, and tanks. We even joke about death.

Mariupol is the only thing we don't joke about.

Why? Well, you must have guessed it already. Because when

parents bury their children, the joke just doesn't ring right.

Children dying is a strike no one is ever prepared for. No, not 'dying'. Because it's not like they get sick and wither in a hospital. It's not like they die in a car accident. They are being killed (isn't it crazy how you can use present tense in a sentence like this?).

I see that I fail to conjure the words sufficient to describe my dissonance. When you read about a child dying in a faraway country, it always feels unreal, fictional. How do I explain what it feels like when it is right here?

If you have children, I implore you to make an experiment, albeit a cruel one.

1. Wait for your kid to go to sleep.

2. Take their hand into yours so that it fits right inside.

3. Understand how much smaller their hand is compared to yours.

4. Think of what you are prepared to do in order for your child to be alive.

5. Comprehend that when war comes, all of the things you thought of in point 4 are useless. You are not going to fight off a bomb. You are not faster than a plane. You will be nothing more than a mourner.

The Mariupol Drama Theatre wasn't just another bomb shelter. It sheltered the very soul of the city—the smallest, the weakest, the most precious. The future. The children. Those who have been protected by the unwritten rules of war throughout history. For Russians, though, the word 'bomb' and the word 'children' fit in one sentence just fine.

Please, burn it into your minds: some very rich and very powerful men built the most dangerous and destructive weapons of this age and killed children with them. How does the world make any sense after this? How do you go about your business knowing this?

And I want you to understand this perfectly: the word 'CHILDREN' was laid on 9 by 30 meters of ground outside the theatre. The two repeating words were impossible to miss from a plane. The Russian pilot knew there were kids there. And he dropped the bomb. Not despite the presence of children, but because of that. He did it deliberately. Purposefully. With the intent to kill the little people who barely understood what a bomb was, because the world they had lived in was devoid of war.

This was not a misunderstanding, this was not a tragic mistake. This was strategy. To despair your opponent into surrender. It is the same strategy the Russians adopted in Chechnya, Georgia, Afghanistan, Syria. But never again. Ukraine is their final mistake. They lost the very moment they stepped foot in my country.

So why Mariupol, you ask?

It was revenge. Revenge for defiance. You see, this was supposed to be the most pro-Russian city in Ukraine. They thought they would be greeted as liberators. With bread and salt and flowers. And they weren't.

Mariupol was almost rebuilt anew after the Russian onslaught of 2014. And it was beautiful. Because everything truly Ukrainian is beautiful. And this was revenge for being beautiful.

Thus, the city of formerly 450,000 people is simply no more.

This is what the word 'Mariupol' means now. Something beautiful which is no more. Something that is mutilated out of spite. It represents the feeling of loss and despair. And so much anger, it could drown the horizon.

"NO ONE CAN SERVE TWO MASTERS": PROBLEMS WITH UKRAINIAN-RUSSIAN BILINGUALISM

Iryna Ivankovych

While the notion of bilingualism bears no universal harm, there is something profoundly wrong with Ukrainian-Russian code switching. The idea of the Russian language and cultural supremacy over the Ukrainian has deeply permeated in the minds of my many fellow countrymen who succumbed to the pseudo-grandeur of the 'older brother' (старший брат). One has to remember that the Russian empire issued over one hundred decrees (e.g. Valuyev and Emsk decrees) aimed at complete Russification of Ukraine, and thus, killing the Ukrainian language, culture, and spirit. With the two uprisings: The Orange Revolution of 2004, and the Revolution of Dignity of 2013-2014, the situation began to change. Slowly, sometimes painfully. The inferiority complex of the 'little Russian' (малорос) seemed to be weakening. More and more people consciously chose Ukrainian as their language. Yet, the majority were still looking back at mother Russia as an epitome of splendor and magnificence of its seemingly great language, literature, culture and stolen history. The war has sharpened the necessity of linguistic identification. It challenges people to face their 'linguistic schizophrenia.' Speaking from experience, the process is complex, tough, and doable.

I grew up in a bilingual family. My father hailed from Lithuanian, Ukrainian and Belarusian families. In his heart, however, he was always a hard-core Russian. Born in Siberia, where my ancestors were sent for being 'the enemies of the Soviet regime,' he was brainwashed by Russian propaganda. Having served the term, my grandparents moved to Donbas, and my father grew up in an entirely Russian-speaking community—one of people who washed off their national identities. My mother comes from a family of Ukrainians, Poles and Austrians residing in Halychyna (Galicia, Western Ukraine). In her heart and soul, she has always been Ukrainian. The union of the two was an unlikely duo: A Soviet-regime-lover and a Soviet-regime-hater.

As a child, I associated language (мова) and "tongue" (язык) with one of my parents. Dad (or rather "Papa") instilled everything Russian in me: poems, songs, fairy tales, etc. And because in those dark, Soviet times they were in abundance, I easily picked up everything that my father's channels transmuted. My mother and my mom's mother taught me Ukrainian songs, fairy tales, poems, and legends. It was my "Secret Garden," where this profound Ukrainian spirit seemed almost an enigma. Trips to my father's family in Horlivka, Donbas region, left memories of pitch-black heaps, delicious ice cream, and drunken residents of the nine-story building where my father's parents lived. Childhood in the house of my mom's parents was "a cherry orchard by the house," as Ukrainian poet Taras Shevchenko would say.

My school years exacerbated this bifurcation. Our Ukrainian-language school in Ternopil opened a class for the in-depth study of the Russian language. Of course, as a 'half-Russian', my father commanded me to take it. Russian literature was filled with the spirit of the nobility of the Onegins, Rostovs, and the elegance of Akhmatova. The Ukrainian literature classes presented boring misinterpretations of two of the greatest Ukrainian writers—Taras Shevchenko and Ivan Franko—as leaders of socialism among the oppressed, uneducated peasants who could only be saved by the Russians.

I vividly remember Lesya Ukrainka's "The Forest Song": that was probably the turning point for my already split personality. At that time, Alexander Pushkin's "Eugene Onegin" and the abovementioned "The Forest Song" were staged at the school. I had to choose between the role of Tatiana Larina and Mavka. Intuitively, I chose Mavka. It was the end of the 80's: a lot was changing in people's minds. However, this choice cost me an A+ in Russian and a Valedictorian award. But the play was a pure pleasure.

At that time, the identity of the Ukrainian had already crystallized in me. When receiving my first ID, I chose 'Ukrainian' in the nationality section, to my father's dissatisfaction and my mother's joy. Leaving for college in Poland, I was already deeply in love with Ukraine's history, culture, language, and literature. It is fitting to pay tribute to my mother: in those difficult years she did not spare a meager salary for the then-rare books by Mykhailo Hrushevsky, Vasyl Stus, Lina Kostenko, Vasyl Symonenko, Bohdan Lepky, Oleksandr Oles, Olena Teliha, and other Ukrainian scholars and writers prohibited by the Soviet regime.

My years of emigration put the Russian language into the back burner. With my father's absence and subsequent death, there was no more pressure to use that language. With the events of 2004, and 2013-14, the feeling of rejection towards everything Russian intensified. The part of me that my father's family tried to raise in the Russian spirit rested in peace.

I have come a long way from fascination with the Russian realm to having a next-to-allergic reaction to everything this realm creates. One should not comfort themselves with the concept of harmless Ukrainian-Russian bilingualism: it simply cannot be such for political and historical reasons. We are not in Canada or Switzerland, although even they cannot claim the 100% success of bilingualism. One 'hemisphere' of the personality will always prevail. Today, when the war is ravaging over Ukraine, claiming the lives of thousands, the choice is there for every bilingual citizen of the country: Which of these hemispheres will dominate? Who will we get out of this war: people diagnosed with "language schizophrenia" or people who, in addition to their native language, can speak their enemy's? "No one can serve two masters" (Matthew 6:24).

Про мову і не тільки: «не можна служити двом панам»

У мене щораз частіше з'являється алергічна реакція на «вєлікій могучій». На це багато причин, але про них не сьогодні. Нині про двомовність (укр-рос.) або мовну шизофренію

Я виросла у двомовній родині. Мій батько - у рівному співвідношенні литовець, білорус та українець. У паспорті і за переконанням - русский. Народжений в Сибіру (причину, гадаю, не потрібно з'ясовувати), виріс на Донбасі. Мама з родини українців, поляків та австрійців Галичини. У серці - українка. Ось такий собі тандем Сходу і Заходу.

Змалечку мова і «язик» асоціювалися у мене з одним із батьків. Тато (вірніше «папа») вщеплював усе російське: вірші, пісні, казки, тощо. А що у ті темні, совєтські часи цього добра було більш ніж достатньо, я легко підхоплювала усе, що «транслювали» «гени» батька. Мама і бабуся навчали українських пісень, казок, віршів, переказів і то був наче такий «Secret Garden», де весь отой пласт українства здавався майже енігмою. Поїздки в родинну Горлівку батька залишали спогади териконів, морозива і нетверезих мешканців дев'ятиповерхівки, де жили батьки тата. Дитинство у домі дідуся і бабусі - це наче «садок вишневий коло хати»

Шкільні роки загострили це «роздвоєння», коли у нашій україномовній школі відкрили клас з поглибленим вивченням російської мови. Зрозуміло, моє місце було там. Російська література була наповнена духом дворянства Онєгіних, Ростових, витонченістю Ахматової. Українська - схибленою інтерпретацією Шевченка та Франка борців за соціалізм (Боже, який маразм). Тільки Лесину «Лісову пісню» пригадую дуже чітко, бо то, мабуть, була зворотня точка у моїй уже доволі роздвоєній особистості. Тоді у школі паралельно ставили «Онєгіна» і «Лісову пісню». Вибір став між роллю Татьяни Ларіноі і Мавкою. Я інтуїтивно обрала Мавку. То був уже кінець 80-х, багато що мінялося у свідомості людей. Однак цей вибір коштував мене відмінної оцінки з російської мови і золотої медалі. Зате яке задоволення від п'єси!

Тоді уже чітко скристалізувалася в мені тотожність українки і це відповідно було зафіксовано у паспорті, попри невдоволення батька. На навчання до Польщі їхала дівчина, закохана в історію, культуру, мову і літературу свого народу. Мушу віддати належне моїй мамі: у ті важкі роки вона не щадила скупої зарплати на раритетні тоді книги Грушевського, Стуса, Костенко, Симоненка, Лепкого.

Роки на еміграції відсунули на другий план необхідність російської. Батька не було, потім не стало, тому і в родинному колі тиск вживати «язик» зник. А мій язик наче засох. З подіями 2004, 2013-14 загострилося відчуття відторгнення (і каменуйте мене психолінгвісти!) до усього російського. Та частина мене, яку намагалися виховати в російському дусі, остаточно вмерла.

До чого це я? Не варто втішати себе поняттям нешкідливої двомовності. У випадку українсько-русского тандему її не може бути з причин політичних та історичних. Ми не в Канаді чи Швейцарії, хоча і там годі говорити про стовідсотковий успіх білінгвальности. Завжди переважатиме одна «півкуля» особистості. Сьогодні, в умовах війни, вибір за кожним двомовним громадянином України: яка із цих півкуль домінуватиме? Ким ми вийдемо з цієї війни: людьми з діагнозом «мовної шизофренії», чи людьми, які, окрім рідної, знають мову ворога?

STORM CLOUDS ABOVE UKRAINE

Larysa Martyniuk

DAYDREAMING

Kateryna Voloshyna

Kira was sitting in anticipation of the most delicious coffee in Lviv City. At that moment, it seemed to her that only she knew this secret, she owned the key to happiness, the door to a coffee shop where a magical drink was served, turning any gray autumn rainy day into something filled with hope and reflection on adventures. She did not have to strain her eyesight, to be able to quietly watch the lone tourists on the right side, who from time to time pulled on the front door to the tiny chapel, checking their luck. Yet, luck was not often on their side, and only a few of them still managed to wait for the museum curator to come and open the door so they could look at the remnants of the old era made completely in black color.

Each year Kira herself was knocking and pulling this door several times, trying again and again to get into a mysterious little hiding place from tourists and the sun that was too bright. But this autumn day she was in no hurry. After several years of annual visits to Lviv, she could proudly note that she had been to the chapel exactly two times, and the third time she looked into the hole, from behind Polish tourists.

A cheerful waitress has finally brought the coffee. Kira slipped in a soft chair woven from a vine or maybe a palm tree. She grabbed a woolen plaid in red and black colors from an empty chair. Blowing on her coffee several times, she sipped the dark hot liquid. Perhaps, it would be better to order the strawberry cake, which the waiters offered her several times. Kira looked up and scanned the almost empty stone street. Opposite to her, behind an iron fence, stood a Saint made of stone. The pale color of stone which the Saint was made of stood out against the darker street, also flooded by the rain. The statue of the Saint must have been even brighter once, a long time ago, while someone's hands created him. He looked sadly at Kira from behind the fence. Kira looked at him happily. She liked the feeling of comfort that engulfed her.

A cool autumn rain dripped on the street, almost at arm's length from her. It washed away the summer heat and the presence of a crowd. The sky had acquired an incredible mix of blue and gray, and it seemed that the bush behind the fence where this Saint with a sad face stood had become even greener, even juicier. In the church, of which this Saint was a part, the light burned comfortably. It made its way through the elongated, arched windows, and illuminated part of the street, and Kira's mood. Her coffee cooled a little, allowing Kira to take larger sips. She wrapped herself into plaid tightly. All her thoughts about life, reflections on work, family, and her own achievements were gone, disappearing at the moment. Probably this rain washed them away. Kira was completely focused on the Saint, who stood behind the fence for many years, much longer than one decade, and on the rain, which washed the Saint's face. All this came before her, and it would remain when she was gone. A stone road, a fence, a Saint peering over it, a tiny chapel on top of which Jesus, green from time immemorial, sat down to rest. They all cared little about her problems. Kira smiled. She wished to sit like this forever, drinking coffee in the rain, wrapped in a blanket.

For some reason, another cozy day came to her mind. Kira had been in high school. She was not a sophomore yet and could relax a bit because exams were ahead of her, and thoughts about university could be postponed until next year. She was sitting in the corner of the class, by the window on the front desk, fascinated by the green-brown leaves of huge chestnuts in the small school park. It was the last lesson. And after that, she could run home and watch Charmed on TV until her friends called her for a walk. Kira would usually be occupied with clubs or homework, but it was a Friday. The sun lazily illuminated half of the room, just from Kira's side.

Her favorite teacher of Ukrainian literature came to class. The bell had not yet rung, and she could talk to the girls gathered around her. The teacher said that her daughter, who was already an adult, and by Kira's standards a respectable lady because she was a third-year student at the university, went to the Vatican via a student program. Kira had no clue of this Vatican, but she knew that it was somewhere far abroad, somewhere in her dreams, which will probably never come true. After all, who travels abroad in Ukraine? Kira listened to the story and looked at the green, slightly toasted chestnut leaves. The hot sun warmed her hands, reflected in the dark brown lacquer of the desk. It was then that Kira first realized that in her life there would be travels, adventures, and everything she wanted if she worked without stopping. All she had to do was start dreaming!

THE FAMILY GRAVEYARD

Dr. Nazarii Nazariv

How was it then
to live under the clouds
beneath the sky
unchecked by the horizon?
travelling through the nights
all by moonlight
all by one's self
confronting no one but distance?

Fetching water from wells
fish from the rivers
silence from fields
hay from under a willow

And who would have told you
that you'd live
in whisper in darkness in wind
in evening in shadows
in willows
but never again as a human
For your life outstretched the horizon
went beyond the stars
back then long ago
before I met you
in the silence of the family graveyard

A DEWDROP IN THE OCEAN

Sofiia Tiapkina

Now it was many moons ago that mavkas came to Earth. Towards the east and also southward, towards the west and also northward, they traverse Ukrainian lands. Mavkas are a springlet's laughter, a birch's song, a stone's whisper. The Sky is their father, and the Earth cradles them like no mother before. Sometimes they use their honey-voices to lure young men into marshes and moss-filled hollows. Sometimes they just wander in their realm, unseen, unheard, undiscovered.

Spring has always been the favorite of Rosynka. The Earth's tiny fingers and toes start bursting through in green and white. Every time the sun's smile creeps up the horizon, she goes out to the fields, for Rosynka is the guardian of dew. A poppy petal, a sunflower stem, an oak leaf, all receive her sweet moisture.

When the grass reaches her knees, Rosynka starts finding treats in the meadows—a loaf of bread and a jug of milk. Shepherds don't forget the kind guardian who keeps their pastures lush and cows fed. No wonder people say: "Rosynka feeds children milk." And how she loves to watch the little ones play in the steppe!

Today there is no laughter under the Sky. The fisherman didn't come to his slip. She asks the thornbush, the wheat, the lake by the aspen. She runs to the village, forgetting that the gray crones would set her on fire if they saw her near men. A nimble breeze, she swirls further and further, down the empty roads and past the dark windows. Somewhere here, she remembers, there must be…

A pit.

A pit, Earth with her insides out, in the place of a pretty white building with a poplar nearby where the little ones spent most of their days.

"Why… where did you go?" Rosynka whispers to the devastated ground. The building, the poplar, the little ones. Where?

Only yesterday, she saw them running out to their parents, hugging and babbling about their day. They were dyeing eggs for the Velukden, asking their mothers if they had already baked the Paska. Rosynka remembers how the little ones loved Easter. Ringing the bells, crashing the eggs, singing with the whole village. She heard their voices through the darkness of the night.

Where are they? Rosynka moves away from the tortured Earth. In her haste, she stumbles over something, a twig, a rock? No, Rosynka looks into a dusted face. The pup is just lying there, not moving even as she reaches out to bury her hands in the dirty hair. Perhaps it is dead. Perhaps it feels dead, wants to be. Rosynka saw how animals pretend, hoping to survive an attack. Perhaps this one is like the others, stunned with fear, unable to move. Alive but dead.

"Stand up," she says. "Stand up and run. Find your parents. Go!"

But he stays on the ground. His fingers are claws on Rosynka's hand. She shakes him, hugs him, takes him in her arms. He feels heavy, more like a dog than a puppy. She smooths the hair out of his eyes.

They round the corner to the outskirts of the village. The river that flowed along it turned into black sludge. Where are the storks, the crayfish? The fisherman who played the sopilka on the cool mornings? He always smiled when Rosynka hid behind birches to hear the sad melody.

"They are not coming back, are they?"

The world is silent except for the whimpers of the thing in her arms.

She must save it. A rumbling grows from the fields and rams in a blast of fire into the village. She falls to the ground, envelopes him in her arms, trembling with the Earth beneath her. Her eyes feel wet. Why, Rosynka only ever cried for the red kalyna, for the shepherds and the little ones, for the Sky and the Earth. She lets the dewdrops fall into the black soil.

The rumbling is closer, darker, colder. A strange bolder, or a stick, a caterpillar? A monster is coming up the herders' road. Rosynka wants to stand up, to run, to hide this thing crying into her shirt. But her legs feel numb. Maybe the animal inside her is also lifeless, no power to protect itself. A ghost of will.

"No… no, that's not how it ends." Rosynka feels sky-blue blood on her fingertips. The villagers lived through the bitter freeze, floods, wildfire, and famine. Mavkas come and go, back to the skysill when their time comes. But they, the people, are tenacious. The will to live would never leave them, even if you beat them with sticks, stones, or firebolts. The grief only makes them stronger. And furious. They will live.

She comes up to her knees; her left leg is a mash of lilac-blue-gold. She puts the child behind her back, clutches him with all her strength.

The monster is here, on her land. It will know Hell.

WATERCOLOR MAVKA

Sofiia Tiapkina

THIS POEM IS LASTING WHILE THE WAR IS LASTING

Victoria Feshchuk, translated by Odarka Bilokon

Day 1
To grab your cat in time
to hold on to a news feed
all the way long.

Day 2
Right after the alert
boys are afraid of a new invasion
girls keep silent.

Day 3
After a curfew
no pads are left
war does not have a woman's face.

Day 4
From a siren to siren
you have time to clean the floor
it will get covered or get dry.

Day 5
Now you are afraid to wash your head for long

to stay naked and soaped
under a threat of an air raid.

Day 6
To hear no fear on my mom's side
to show no fear to her
to talk three times a day.

Day 7
To sleep in a tracksuit
to sleep under any circumstances
to sleep.

Day 8
News about rape cases
in Kherson were not confirmed
they promise the next negotiation.

Day 9
The girl from Kharkiv whom I know says
the ordinary thing is to be unable to save
a human next to you.

Day 10
My friend is charmed
looking at a rifle of a local guard
you cannot get to Kyiv now.

Day 11
My other friend, almost a sister

is out of contact for more than a week
our wrath is not enough.

Day 12
My friend says it's hard to pronounce when
everything's over as the war is still going on
pauses for sleep are insecure.

Day 13
My grandma asks her deceased relatives
to save the land
the land keeps silent.

Day 14
I had a lovely dream
for the first time in two months
is it all clear?

Day 15
We've missed sirens
when buying cottage cheese at the fair
it's going to be a cheese bake.

Day 16
After the alert in the cellar
slugs are crawling to the light
they feel the spring is coming.

Day 17
A siren is screaming with rage

and the neighbor's dog
got used to stealing eggs.

Day 18
Today we've harvested potatoes
like it's a holiday. We had
the whole day without the war.

Day 19
It's closer to the ground from here
than anywhere else.
So we're staying here.

Day 20
Neighbors cry the war out
they blame sounds for everything,
this is how we've watched the sunrise.

Цей вірш триває поки триває війна

день 1
вчасно схопити кота
триматись за стрічку новин
усю дорогу.

день 2
після тривоги
хлопці бояться нового вторгнення
дівчата - мовчать.

день 3
по комендантській годині
зовсім не лишилось прокладок
у війни не жіноче обличчя.

день 4
від сирени і до сирени
встигаєш помити підлогу
або засипле або висохне.

день 5
а тепер боїшся довго милити голову
лишитися голою і намиленою
при загрозі авіаудару.

день 6
не почути від мами страху
не показати свого
говорити тричі на день.

день 7
спати в спортивнім костюмі
спати за будь-яких умов
спати.

день 8
звістки про зґвалтування дівчат
із херсону не підтвердились
обіцяють чергові перемовини.

день 9
знайома з харкова каже
буденність це не вміти рятувати
людину поруч.

день 10
подруга заворожено
дивиться на рушницю місцевої охорони
а до києва зараз не дістатися.

день 11
інша подруга майже сестра
не виходить на зв'язок більше тижня
нашого гніву не достатньо.

день 12
подруга каже: важко вимовляти коли
все закінчиться бо війна триває
паузи на сни ненадійні.

день 13
бабця просить мертвих родичів
берегти землю
земля мовчить.

день 14
наснився добрий сон
уперше за два місяці
відбій тривоги?

день 15
пропустили сирени купуючи
сир на ярмарку
запіканці бути.

день 16
після тривоги у погребі
слимаки повзуть на світло
передчувають весну.

день 17
сирена гуде гнівом
а наш сусідський пес
унадився красти яйця.

день 18
сьогодні вбирали картоплі
як на свято. мали собі
цілий день без війни.

день 19
звідси ближче до землі
ніж куди небудь.
тут і лишаємось.

день 20
сусіди викрикують війну
звинувачують звуки у всьому
так ми зустріли світанок

LIFE WILL DEFEAT DEATH

Olena Prygoda

UNTITLED

Halyna Kruk, translated by R.B. Lemberg

You stand with your little "No war" sign like it's your atonement
for what can't be reversed now: the war can't be stopped,
like bright blood from a torn artery—
it gushes forcefully, draining energy and life,
bursts into our cities as armed soldiers,
scatters its sabotage groups in the inner courtyards,
like deadly mercury balls that can't be gathered up,
can't be turned back, only tracked and neutralized
by those civilians—managers, clerks, IT workers, students,
whose life didn't prepare them for street battles, but the war teaches
rapidly, in field conditions, on this painfully familiar ground
territorial defenses first took men with combat experience,
then, even those whose combat experience was Dune and Fallout
and a short masterclass in explosive cocktails from a friendly
bartender. In the nearest nightclub,
children are sleeping, children are crying, children are born
into this world temporarily unfit for life
in the courtyard by the playground, the anti-tank hedgehogs
and deadly "drinks" are being poured—now a family business
for the whole kin, who learned, at last, the joy of togetherness
and of coordinated collective labor—war shortens the distance
between one person and the next, between birth and death,

between what we didn't want for ourselves
and what we were capable of doing
—mom, pick up the phone,—begs the woman
in the basement of a high-rise, for the second hour already,
stubbornly, numbly, never ceasing to believe in miracles
but her mom is beyond reach, in that little town
where walls melted down like cheap Legos
from mass strikes, where already last night, the network towers
stopped working, where the world
was torn into before and after the war
along the uneven fold of your little "no war" sign
which you'll toss into the nearest trash can
walking home from the protests, you, Russian poet
War kills with the hands of the indifferent
and even with the hands of passive sympathizers

стоїш із плакатиком "no war" як індульгенцією за те,

чого уже не відвернути: війну не зупинити,
як яскраву кров із розірваної артерії—
вона тече стрімко, позбавляючи сил і життя,
вона заходить у наші міста озброєними людьми,
розсипається ворожими дрг у внутрішніх дворах,
ніби смертельні ртутні кульки, що їх уже не визбирати,
не повернути назад, хіба що вистежувати і знешкоджувати
цим цивільним менеджерам, клеркам, айтішникам і студентам,
яких життя не готувало до вуличних боїв, але війна вчить
в польових умовах, на до болю знайомій місцевості, наспіх
в тероборону спершу беруть чоловіків із бойовим досвідом,

потім уже навіть тих, що мають за плечима тільки Dune і
Fallout,
ну і ще короткий майстерклас із приготування вибухових
коктейлів
від знайомого бармена. в найближчого нічному клубі
сплять діти, плачуть діти, народжуються діти
у світ, тимчасово непридатний для життя
у дворі на дитячому майданчику варять протитанкові їжаки
і розливають смертельні "напої"—сімейним підрядом,
цілими родинами, які нарешті спізнали радість спілкування
і злагодженої колективної праці—війна скорочує відстань
від людини до людини, від народження до смерті,
від того, чого ми собі не бажали—до того, на що ми виявилися
здатні
—мамо, візьми трубку,—другу годину просить жінка
у підвалі багатоповерхівки, вперто і глухо,
не припиняючи вірити в чудо
але мама її поза зоною досяжності, у тому передмісті,
де панельки склалися, як дешевий конструктор,
від масованих ударів, де вежі зв'язку ще вчора
перестали зв'язувати, де світ розірвався на до війни і після
вздовж нерівного згину плакатика "no war",
який ти викинеш у найближчий смітник,
ідучи із протестів додому, російський поете
війна убиває руками байдужих
і навіть руками бездіяльних співчутливих

ACKNOWLEDGMENT: We want to thank CHYTOMO for facilitating the Ukrainian poem and its translation to IHRAF. CHYTOMO is an independent media covering publishing and contemporary

literary and cultural processes in Ukraine.
Website: *www.chytomo.com/e*

VERTIGO IN THE 21ST CENTURY

Askold Skalsky

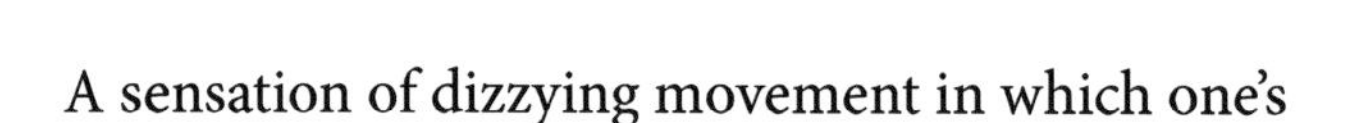

A sensation of dizzying movement in which one's
surroundings seem to whirl.

After the first war there is no other, only a desperate bestiary
of ruined forms, botches of shot-out windows and emaciated
walls among the reeds. We launch the holy missiles of experience,
raiding the sacristy of what's left of every shell and shelling,
high and low, a bead without its rosary, a parsonage devoid
of grace and mystery, seeking the bombed-out bistros of
our storied dreams, their substance rubbled into illusion's trench
beneath the battered housetops and every lair of ordinanced
depravity—armed lizards with serpent heads, drawn by sirens
of aborted earth and the steely crawl of their artilleries.
For we struggle not for bread and flesh but for light in the high
places of our hidden hearts while the smell of paraffin is strong
and the booming flares appear like hellish rivers ransacking
their banks and spilling into brimful cemetery plots.
Mine eyes have seen
the flux and reflux of the Lord
dawdling in the desert
with his cauterizing sword
And the dead go marching on.

PAIN

Olena Prygoda

THE WOLF HOUR

Ella Yevtushenko

I.

the hour between 3 am and 4 am
is called the wolf hour in Sweden
when it is too late to fall asleep
and too early to get up
so they stay in bed listening
to (their mental) wolves
this is how Ullmar explained it

the curfew in Kyiv is
from 8 pm till 7 am
the curfew in Kherson is
from 8 pm till 6 am
the curfew in Kharkiv is
from 4 pm till 6 am
when it is too late to die
but too early to live
so we stay in bed guessing
what are these sounds: they bombing us or
we are taking down their missiles
and no one can ever explain any of this

II.

in 35 years in Chernobyl Exclusion Zone
the population of wolves has increased
and now a bear has been spotted here
the most dangerous of all large predators
it came here from the territory of Belarus
this is how Serhiy Hashchak, the researcher of the fauna
in the exclusion zone, explained it

this spring, great fires are expected here
but nature is able to restore itself
explained Mr. Hashchak
the pictures from camera traps show
how the fire is roaring and local inhabitants are fleeing to the west
but in a month, green grass will be sprouting here
and young deer and moose will be grazing

but the time has not come yet. It is still cold
the wolves gather in large packs for hunting
at the wolf hour
they will take on their thermal cameras
strong and ardent, they will go
and you know what
together they will hunt down the bear
and this will be very easy to explain

вовча година

I.

з третьої ночі до четвертої ранку
у Швеції триває вовча година
коли запізно аби заснути
але зарано аби звестися з ліжка
і ти лежиш дослухаючись
до (своїх внутрішніх) вовків
так пояснив мені Ульмар

з восьмої вечора до сьомої ранку
у Києві триває комендантська година
з восьмої вечора до шостої ранку
у Херсона триває комендантська година
з четвертої дня до шостої ранку
у Харкові триває комендантська година
коли запізно аби померти
але зарано аби жити
і ти лежиш дослухаючись
це нас бомблять чи наші збивають
і все це годі комусь пояснити

II.

за тридцять п'ять років у Чорнобильській зоні
відновилася популяція вовків
а тепер тут зафіксували ведмедя
найбільш небезпечного з великих хижаків
він зайшов сюди з білоруської території
так пояснив Сергій Гащак, дослідник фауни в зоні відчуження

цієї весни тут очікують великі пожежі
але природа вміє відновлюватися
пояснив пан Гащак
на кадрах фотопасток видно
як вирує вогонь і тікають на захід тутешні мешканці
але вже за місяць тут ростиме зелена трава
і пастимуться молоді олені й лосі

але поки не час поки ще холодно
вовки збираються на полювання у великі зграї
о вовчій годині ночі
вони надягнуть тепловізори
підуть міцні та завзяті
і знаєте що
гуртом уполюють ведмедя
і якраз-таки це буде дуже легко пояснити

WAITING

Tatyana Shramko

280 WORDS

Lex Shramko

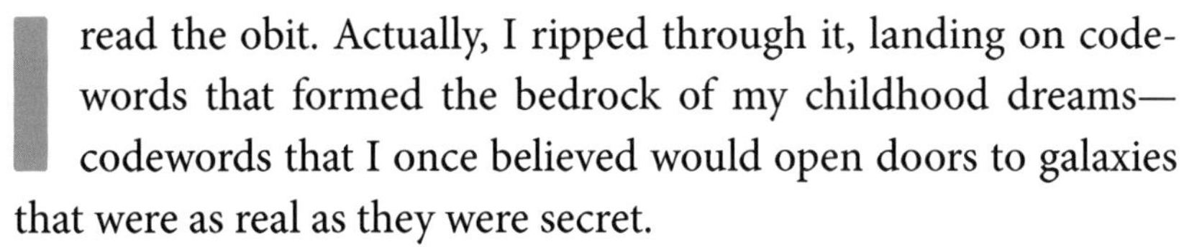

I read the obit. Actually, I ripped through it, landing on codewords that formed the bedrock of my childhood dreams—codewords that I once believed would open doors to galaxies that were as real as they were secret.

I was looking at a thumbnail photo of my mother's sister, missing for 69 years from my mother's life and all of mine. In her absence, I had a few stories and even fewer names. Definitely no records or photos. When my mother and her sister were separated at some unknown German border in May of 1945, they each had only their memories and the ragged clothes they wore. My mother was 11 years old, and Galina was 23.

Now, close to midnight on a Thursday in early October, 2014, I was holding her image in my hands.

Born in Manchuria.
"Manchuria." Our secret word, a unique geopolitical lexicon.

Survived Stalin and lost all her family.
"Stalin killed your grandfather!" Her family, too, was lost.

Walked through Europe.
Two years walking with too-small shoes. My mother's hammer toes.

Had a daughter named Tatjana
My mother's name is Tatyana.

Her famous 16-foot Christmas trees.
Our 14-foot Christmas trees. My mother on a ladder.

Where is her sister, Tatyana S.
My mother's name. Slightly varied, but hers. And hers alone.

Is this happening? Is this real? It is real but also not real. It's real at the level below your brain but the level below your brain doesn't have words for it. The realm of embodied cognition doesn't have language, yet it's the oldest form of knowing.

At this moment, I have six years' distance from that night, from that experience of finding. Today, when I re-read the obituary, I marvel at how brief it is. Fifteen sentences and 280 words. When I first encountered it, I was transported to another world where time slowed and space contracted, where 280 words projected on some kind of astral plane and made real another place, time, and reality. I was still on this earth, and yet, for the briefest moment, also not of this earth. And I wanted to stay exactly right there.

It is, perhaps, an odd place to want to stay. Here, two opposing experiences collide. One experience was a joyous discovery: finding something that was once lost. The other experience was the pain of loss through death. Taken together, this is the experience of finding something only to simultaneously lose it again.

I had grown up with a ghost whom I had always wanted to find and make living flesh, to restore to my mother. Instead here I was, with a dead ghost. I held her obituary in my hands, late at night at that portentous midnight hour, and I was in shock. And yet I wanted to stay right there, suspended in a state of unreality where all my mother's stories were not only true, they also had an echo. Someone else grew up with these stories, too.

For the better part of my nearly 40 years, this missing ghost that had tickled around in my genes, summonable with a silent thought-word in my head ("Manchuria," with the rolled 'r' and the long 'u'), was now found, and about to be made (dead) flesh.

Although I had found her, I was going to miss her. And before I called my mother, I stroked her face in the photo, feeling the glass under my fingertip and saying to myself, "you're my kin, aren't you?"

• • •

There was no question, I had to reach my mom in Washington, DC. She was barely home a week from surgery (we were awaiting the results from pathology), and I had just returned to Pennsylvania. Disturbing her was probably not good for her health, but this could not wait.

My cochlear implant processors sat by my bed, powered down. Sliding one over my right ear—my better ear—I called my mother's cell phone and got voicemail. I disconnected.

I called the house phone and let it ring. Each unanswered ring echoed in my head, an audiological after-glare humming in my inner ears. I disconnected and rang her cell again. Still no answer. My third phone call was to the house phone, my fourth call to her cell. Back and forth, back and forth, between the audible house phone and the vibrating cell phone. My mom's voice, heavy with sleep, answered my seventh call.

"Yes? What is it?" Weary but warm and soothing. She knew something was up and I hesitated, searching for the right words through the chaos of emotions. I threw my voice into the dark, asking for my mom. I needed her, and I understood too that she needed me.

"Mom?"

"Yes?"

"I found Galina."

• • •

There was, of course, that stunned pause. Language—our capacities for words and meaning and syntax and rules and order—that nifty little human trick—was completely shattered, as if by a tsunami slamming onto a coastline. Together, we groped for the meanings of words.

Over the thin line of our telephone connection, I waited for her response. I sat, folded, on the arm of the couch. I rested my elbows on my knees and locked the phone into place on my ear, precisely lining up the phone's speaker to my processor's mic. A line of connectivity between us.

Tears streamed down my face, dripped onto my pajama pants, and soaked through to my skin. In the gap of waiting silence, I listened to her stunned awakening, her hope, her joy, her pain. Balanced on the rail of our phone call, I felt the kaleidoscope of her emotions unfurl and blossom.

We hung for a moment, suspended between the sweetness of finding what was lost, and the grief of finding the dead.

"Quick-tell-me-is-she-dead-or-alive?"

My tsunami of grief tumbled down the phone line, chasing away hope and killing joy. I heard her mouth open to speak into my stuttered silence, and I drew in the air needed to drive my voice forward. She had been waiting for this answer for the better part of 70 years.

"Mom, I'm so sorry, I'm sorry. She's dead. I found her obituary."

Silence reverberated down the phone line. She was completely still.

"What—where—how?" Her voice tolled, each word surrounded by silence.

"Google. I put her name into Google."

I heard the intake of breath. "Oh my god."

"Mom, I have her obituary here. Do you want me to read it to you? Can you listen or do you want me to send it?"

"Read it now. Send it to me. Both—yes. Both. But read it now."

I read slowly. I read the words out loud, leaning on the script, clinging to the typed sentences. "Born in Manchuria," I began.

"Oh my god." She breathed.

Manchuria was my mother's codeword, too.

• • •

We were on the phone long past midnight. For an hour, I didn't move—curled over my knees and phone pinned to my ear, held exactly in the one spot that channeled audio most clearly. I re-read the obituary to her. She had questions: where was this funeral home, where was this obituary, did the funeral home have a phone number? What was the daughter's name—how was it spelled? How did I find this obituary? Questions piled out and spilled over the line.

"Mom," I interrupted. "There's a picture here of Galina. Mom, I look like her."

"I know you do," came her reply, its unequivocal tone tickling the electrode in my inner ear and setting off a chorus of ancestral voices in my head. Their ethereal tones soothed, while my heart and gut howled.

"I almost named you after her."

"I know. I remember you telling me that."

• • •

Of those midnight hours after the phone call: I dimly remember we decided that my mother would call the funeral home in the morning, and we headed to our respective beds. I remember the support of the mattress under my back and the crisp texture of the feather comforter around my chin. I could not tell you what thoughts or feelings I had, and I suppose that this is what shock is like. I lay restlessly in bed, utterly awake. My heartbeat, which I cannot hear, was also intangible. I floated stiffly through the witching hours, communing with hope and possibility. A little after five a.m., when the skies tinged grey with the breaking dawn, I finally drifted into a semi-sleep state, mercifully passing the time until nine a.m., the hour of the funeral home's opening.

From bed, I fired an email off to my work, calling in sick. Then I texted my mother, asking if she'd called the funeral home yet. I scrolled through the news. I brushed my teeth. I dressed. Still no response. At nine-thirty, completely beside myself with waiting, I fired off another text, giving my mother twenty minutes to send me an update, or I would call the funeral home myself. I went for a walk. I walked slowly. I felt weak and wobbly and a little sick from the lack of sleep.

Twenty minutes later, a text arrived: "I have called the funeral home and am waiting for them to call back."

I stared at the phone screen. Impatience curdled with exhaustion. I was driven but unable to take action. I had a to-do list a mile long and numerous, urgent, and pressing responsibilities tugging at me.

The phone screen timed out in my hand and flipped to darkness. I stood stock-still on the sidewalk, the chill of October nipping at my bare neck and ears. I didn't know what to think. I flicked the phone on again and re-read the obituary. Was this actually happening? I continued to stand on the sidewalk, unable to go back indoors, and unable to walk anymore. I let the phone time out to darkness and slipped it into my back pocket.

Almost immediately, it vibrated—a text from my mother:

"Alexa. The funeral home called.
and they are contacting
—as they put it—
our family."

Our family.

• • •

Until now, "family" was my dad's side, with my mother as a kind of plus-one. Maternal kinship now unfolded before me as a kind of rare, exquisitely unfamiliar creature. I had no words, no images, no emotions, no abilities to identify what was happening. I didn't just move in a daze; the world around me took on a simultaneous duality of banality and of extra crisp Fuji film saturated hues.

I scrambled to anchor myself. I headed to my favorite sanctuary—a coffee shop. I ordered a cappuccino as if it were the most ordinary thing in the world, but it felt like a miraculous achievement.

Indeed, as I waited in line, my thoughts centered on how this here-and-now moment, in a coffee shop, could arrive and produce a simple, elegantly frothy cappuccino with the little ribboned leaf drawn in the foam. Just imagine how many moving parts had to come together to produce a cappuccino—an enterprising soul needed the desire and the wherewithal to begin a business in a small college town; beans had to be grown in another part of the world, then harvested, bagged, and shipped; a master roaster had to heat and churn the beans; espresso machines had to be engineered and built; business permits obtained; staff found and hired;

brewing methods honed by decades of history; and all of this can only work in a stable, functioning society that can provide shop space for rent and orchestrate insurance policies, and in which an unspoken civil code of conduct oversees a polite queueing up of customers with their wallets open.

Three hours and three cappuccinos later, already over my caffeine limit of two, I had heartburn and no news from my mother despite repeated texts. I moved restlessly to another coffee shop and ordered yet another cappuccino. I hunkered down in a corner seat with my laptop open and distracted myself with work emails and poked at my to-do lists, re-calendaring tasks. I was rigid with impatience, unable to eat. Coffee continued to beckon, as though drinking it would awaken me to my senses.

Midafternoon, my mother sent another text. Her text style in general is a modified haiku with em-dashes—short lines with hard returns to indicate a series of thoughts, all at once. The text that arrived that afternoon appeared to me as an epic-length poem. It felt Homerian, an entire life lived and journeyed, encapsulated in parallel lines to my mother's own story.

Talked with Tatyana
your cousin
for 2plus or 3hrs
they live in Toronto—
husband J—
Galina. lived with them upstairs
two sons one is 22, the second is 26 (I think)
By the way my
sisters husband Nuclear physicist

• • •

Galina had married a physicist. So had my mother.

Galina had had one child—a daughter. So had my mother.

Galina had named her daughter after her missing sister. So had my mother, but with a slight twist: she named me after her missing self.

• • •

Of course, my mother wasn't actually missing to herself, not really. But through a series of (fated?) decisions about what to name me, my middle name ended up being my mother's first name. Initially, Mom considered naming me after Galina, but decided it was important for me to have my own unique name. And, wanting something from her side to pair with my father's family name, she gave me her name. A routine family story, but now, I was suddenly very glad of it.

Time sped up. I fired texts back. When could we meet? Where could we meet? I tapped out all the either/or scenarios. I Googled driving times to Toronto from State College, PA: five hours.

I studied the laptop screen. Canada was much, much further north than a five-hour drive, wasn't it? Five hours. For the last fifteen years I had been living a five-hour drive from my aunt?

I couldn't understand this. And even more bizarre was the fact that my mother's first town as a landed immigrant was Huron, Ohio, just on the other side of Lake Erie from Toronto. We had been hovering on the opposite edges of the same 300-and-some miles nimbus my entire life and never found each other. Understanding the miracle of a frothy cappuccino was much easier for my brain to grasp.

My phone vibrated with a single text from my mother, in reply to the dozens I had sent her. A haiku:

You two are the same!

Both boiling mad to get here

—it's like holding two kittens

You two are the same. Kittens. Sisters. Kin.

INTRODUCTION

Tatyana Shramko

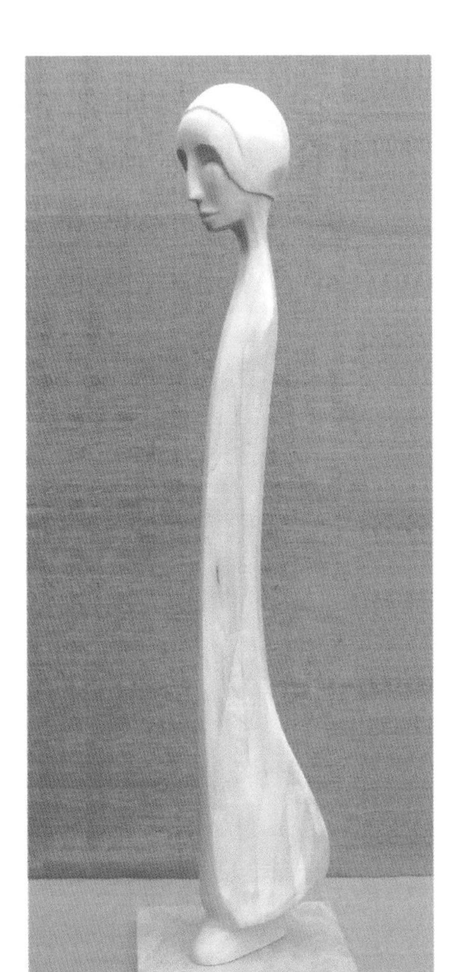

FAMILY BUSINESS

Rimma Kranet

Yana's first husband proposed to her on the way back from a party, while riding in an elevator that crept down from the nineteenth floor like a waterlogged spider. It trembled and swayed, slowly advancing down the narrow shaft. Yellow stains covered the linoleum floor boards and a faint odor of wood shavings and urine inhabited the tight space they shared as they stood close enough to touch, both breathing in the putrid air. He looked down at her cleavage, smiling, and said,

"Your breasts are like two small, ripe apples."

All it took was one observation too intimate to ignore.

Yana surveyed Pavel's shoes. Brown leather consumed the toe, a layer of thick black rubber covering the original thin, delicate soles to protect them from the sleet and cold. Summer shoes made to withstand year-round weather conditions, worn on special occasions, probably bought on the rinok from someone who had managed to smuggle them in from Hungary or Poland. Overall, an ordinary find.

"I think we should get married," Pavel declared, narrowing his brown eyes.

This is what Pavel was: he stood in a suit that had once been his father's, now refurbished and tailored to fit him, the jacket not quite perfect at the shoulders, his whole being just imperfect enough to make Yana feel that he needed her.

They stepped off into a damp evening. A muddy film, slippery and fragrant, glistened in a courtyard where the persistent abuse of children's feet had stunted the growth of what was once newly planted grass. It seemed to be burrowing inward, drowning in the slush, gasping for air with just the tips sprouting to the surface.

Improving the aesthetics of these overbearing housing blocks on the outskirts of town was the only futile effort made by the Soviet Regional Administration to placate the disillusioned residents imploding with anger. Two streets down, Yana's parents shared this same anguish as they gathered in their communal kitchen to discuss the country's troubling state of affairs. Nothing much had changed about this ritual since their youth, except instead of huddling together to read prohibited Western literature and samizdat from exiled Soviet authors, they were washing dishes, smoking and drinking. They had grown into their roles like well planted trees, roots feeding off the rich soil under the watchful eye of Father Stalin.

Pavel's visits became frequent, infusing the kitchen with energy and laughter.

Yana watched as he moved about with ease, cultivating the relationships that most suited the purpose of endearing himself until Yana too became persuaded, no longer procrastinating the inevitable chore of living.

• • •

After less than a year of marriage, Pavel went to Moscow and never came back.

Having waited for three days with no word, Yana called the police.

"It's nothing," the officer she spoke to said, as though he had taken hundreds of such phone calls from panicked women whose husbands had suddenly vanished.

"Give the man a night out. He's probably with his friends in some night spot having a good time. You women are always so uptight. A guy gets married and that's it, his life is over. Go back to sleep—he'll turn up in the morning drunk and happy."

"I don't understand what could have happened to him," Yana insisted.

"Did you have a fight? Did you argue?"

"No, not really.... Can't you do something? Can't you help me look for him?"

"Lady, this is not official business, this is family business. Semeinoe delo... you understand? Taking a break from your wife is not a crime. What's more, it's out of our jurisdiction. You say he's in Moscow... we're in Kiev."

"But he took our money..."

"Ah... does he work?" the police officer asked. He seemed more interested now.

"Yes, he works."

"And do you work?

"No, I mean... not right now. No, I'm not employed, but I have my stipend from the Polytechnic—"

"Well then the man took his own money, right? Wouldn't you say that's fair? You women are incredible... a man can't even do what he likes with his own money...."

The last thing Yana heard through the receiver before hanging up was a chorus of laughter.

• • •

"Men are like household pets. Or zoo animals," Yana's mother said when she came to visit. "They require attention and training. Part of a woman's artistry is knowing when to use her charm, as if it were witchcraft."

Yana's mother looked invariably run down, in a hurry to catch up with life before it slipped out from under her. Her synthetic button down sweaters emanated a faint odor of nervous perspiration, fitting much too snug around her heavy breasts. Her gaze unforgiving, she anxiously drank her tea and shook her head in disbelief. Sitting on the edge of the bed, feet planted firmly on the wooden floorboards, calves touching, her polyester skirt stretched over her knees, she looked like a Soviet poster illustration calling to "Do Your Duty" or "Never Tell a Lie." Words commanding you to deeds that sounded like threats.

• • •

As the days passed, Yana started to notice the neighbors' inquisitive glances in the lobby and on the staircase as she walked up to the apartment she and Pavel shared. Nine square meters per person, that is what the Soviet government deemed worthy of the common man, and that is exactly what Pavel and Yana got along with their marriage certificate and a bottle of the national sparkling wine dubbed champagne. They were a borderline generation split in two, between those who knew how to forge ahead by their wits and those who leapt out of windows on the wrong side of the river, dividing those who could, from those who could not. Perestroika was supposed to bring change, but all it did was endorse survival of the fittest.

• • •

While in line to buy sausage and bread, Yana overheard a man gossiping about someone who had been mugged in the dead of winter by a group of hooligans and suffered a head injury. They took his fur hat and ripped out his gold teeth with nail clippers.

He survived but lost his memory. After some time, a stranger reported him to the police for standing outside their apartment building in his undergarments.

• • •

Yana walked home slowly, the plastic bag filled with groceries weighing her down as she strolled along the river Dnieper. What would people say if they found her drowned, pulled under by strings of pork sausage and a brick of rye bread? She smiled at the image of her body being brought to shore, fingers still tightly wrapped around the handles of her pasty white plastic bag with the faded letters GUM stamped in red across the front. A souvenir from her visit to the famous Moscow department store after her engagement. She should have paid better attention to where they were going back then, to the names of the streets, the places Pavel took her. But how could she have imagined needing that information again? And under such circumstances. In her mind, she had assumed that they would always travel together.

• • •

Making her way, Yana realized that to drown properly she would need an even distribution of weight, therefore she would need two bags filled with groceries, not one. She longed to look inconspicuous, to blend into the crowds of women rushing home to their families at the end of the day. But it would be a shame to spend all of that money on good food only to throw it away. Perhaps she could get canned goods: those were heavier and would not go bad as fast. She knew from listening to the news that steel barrels of tightly packed industrial waste lingered in the dense, sandy bottoms of river beds, silently releasing toxins, polluting the waters around her beloved Ukraine. Surely a bag filled with canned soup would not do such harm.

And what if she was left at the bottom of the river, her body never found? She too would turn into an organic pollutant, dissolving slowly into fish meal.

• • •

Those sharing Yana's landing affectionately suggested she go in person to the district's Police Headquarters to formally initiate an investigation into Pavel's disappearance. The female officer on duty, sitting behind a desk covered in stacks of powder blue protocol folders, greeted Yana with a cordial half smile.

"What happened to you? Were you attacked?"

"No no... Boje upasi... I need to file a report for a missing person."

"Who is missing?" she asked skeptically.

"My husband... it's been three weeks now."

"Are you still waiting for him? Do you know that in Russia, a missing spouse is as common as heart disease? The experts say we'll be abandoned by a man either through divorce, neglect, or domestic violence... read the statistics. Consider yourself lucky. Being a legitimate widow is a luxury—you'll even be entitled to his pension."

"But what if he isn't dead?"

"Don't ask yourself where he is. All you need to know is that he's not with you. You're young; the law says in five years you can file for divorce and remarry. What more do you need?"

From under a console stained with ink, the officer pulled out a "Missing Persons Report" and placed it on the counter. It was a single page with narrow, empty boxes waiting to be filled with Pavel's life. Such a condensed space for the sum of twenty-eight years, Yana thought. If he were older, would she have needed two pages?

"Do you know how many of these we file in the course of one month? Maybe he doesn't want to be found, did that ever occur to you? It happens. But if you insist, we could place your complaint alongside the others who have come before you. It's first come first serve. We lack the manpower to search for everyone who decides not to come home. You think about it and let me know what you want to do. And don't look so glum, I'm giving you a choice."

Yana was indecisive by nature. She stood perplexed, trying to decipher the look on the officer's face, whose expression held no clues.

"Thank you for everything. I will take this with me and think it over." Yana folded the "Missing Persons Report" in half and carefully placed it in her handbag.

"I'm glad we agree. Have a good evening."

Yana walked home under a neon sky leaking shades of blue into the dissolving horizon.

Like in a game of Scrabble, letters formed words that could not settle in Yana's mind. They floated along the edges of her consciousness like the dead leaves of autumn that were swept up by the wind, falling listless into the river Dnieper.

HOME

Stella Hayes

THE RETURN

How do you record illness that is imposed,
that is extra-existential, that is;

that one day you wake up a historically significant
artifact: the brain before a crime.

1.

The linear plainness of the Midwest.
Its vast sprawling endless flatness,
Stretching farther than the eye sees.
Our arrival at O'Hare. We were met

By Father's best friend & his wife. We
Lived with them in fury. They were more
Acclimated to the flat English vowels they
Learned in ESL classes for immigrants.

2.

It was May, the sun was a sunny sun
Looking down on us, Soviet immigrants

Whose belongings were divided into 16 carry-ons,
My mother's brainchild

We transported emptiness & wounds brought
From a country of invented realism, an experiment
In failure possessing the family
Like dispossessed vagabonds

3.
I remember the surface stretching for miles,
Nothing beneath it but a 2-dimensional surface
The depth & sense we left behind with him
In our apartment alongside a wheat field

A cornfield outstretched in The Chicago Tribune
On the front-page Carter's toothy smile espousing
The Wheat for Jews program. Home was an art
Project we left behind with him.

4.
What was their last night together like?
Two bodies, in happiness & sorrow for the last time.
The distance, the night's blanket.
Alternately sleeping & sleepless; the maker of dreams

Making visits. Taking & giving. Eyes closed off.
Lake Michigan became our Dnieper, though deeper, darker
& more distant; its banks drawing in the universe of two. It spat
Us out, it spat. Forgetting the taiga, tundra,

5.

& the steppe's long goodbye. Home is the cave
Cast in long shadows of palms on its walls. In the irrigated
Desert I collect my wounds. My oskolki, pieces of an
Archipelago—making order out of order. Making water

Out of water. Making ocean water
Out of ocean water. Home is the life-long dig unfolding
In daylight. I am digging, where you are the cover, a body
Covering up a home.

PUNISHMENT

6.

I dig up a garden
From poor, rocky soil—a shallow bed for home.
God is existence: a
wound that harmed love's heart.

Don't say mourning. It's too psychoanalytic.
I'm not mourning, I'm suffering
& you are condemned to eyewitness, to breathe,
To put in your arms the one you love

7.

Will always love. Die in his own skin, his death.
There's nothing you can do. My home is green exile. My home
Is knowing I will open the door to our apartment & see him.
The endless pages of the EKGs, the readings of the heart,

The endless readings—the valleys & those high stabs
Of the peaks of the heart, striking you down like the first nail
In a coffin. The depth of depth. The readings of his heart
Were my way into him. Why do you have to go, Father?

8.
I'm alive but you're not—
Each morning is the same: the sun is too bright,
The eyes struck down by blindness. Some sun rays die. One.
Two. Three. Count with me. Won't you? Something you said

Interferes. Trees with their treeness reveal tremors. Absence
Again. Distance again. Nothingness mirroring itself. I repeat
With the precision of knowledge that something is better than
Nothing. As you betray me again. As I betray you again.

9.
We're even,
The trees as blind as us,
Our women grow silent in silence.
I'm going to destroy him—

Because I have nothing better to do.
Razkol, a split of psyche from psyche
You come to faith with all
The will against it that your heart accumulated with eyes

10.
Covered by tired hands. The hands that work with letters,
Smithing them to unfamiliar sounds. Out of step with money,

A church sounding bells on Friday afternoons.
The illness the body endures & will endure

As the past & future meet. Illness with its familiarity
Invades & occupies.
The body laments, the illness the body endures
I sew along the seam of the universe.

11.
In Brovory, a feudal Ukrainian city, he read Solzhenitsyn
In *samizdat.* Dog-eared, thin pages chronicle the empiricism
Of suffering in concentration camps of the Gulag Archipelago.
Tundra forests hiding silence

Concealing longing of one in exile, in longing I weep for him
He was an immigrant for a short time, once an immigrant always
An immigrant with seams like scars unraveling in the open.
A mother tongue became a learned stranger.

THE CAVE
12.
I am a descendant of cave dwellers. The cave that confines
the soul to its body. The borders of trees
Inside it. The borders
Of resemblances of trees outside it.

The cave is like a skin over
The eyes: luminous & opaque.
I will always love my cave
& that nothing resembles it.

13.

Those who remember the cave are ruins. The cave is
a ruin. Distance is the currency of the cave.
The dwellers of the cave measure the world inside it.
They communicate with a light

they cast on the walls of the cave. The light is
estrangement. The light is like light. Remember me
like this. The fire consumes the shadows. I burn
a requiem candle which has no shadow. It burns my reality.

14.

The water boils on the edge of the edge. The borders
on all sides are hot. I serve tea to myself—
A dark fragrance like fragrance
Itself. I'm sipping it at the sipping point,

At the heat point.
I'm not soliciting truth in the slim face of the cave,
A dim light reflected in his eyes
My eyes, her eyes

15.

The self-corrections & self-regulation
& if the world will take its last breath,
I will have to turn away, turn my face to look away
My pajama collection, each in white, is growing.
In more sleep. The way of my survival.

I plan my survival. Each day the plan breaks
down. Each day survival breaks down. But I keep
adding to my collection of white.

16.

In what is the opposite of light, I am contained.
Held. Exiled. Back into the cave.
Why drag yourself out of the shadows cast in gold,
reflecting deep gold, warming up to darkness.

Safely unmoved & unmoving. The warm glow
Of darkness being all there is. *The sun is dead,*
The madman proclaims. & we killed
it. A new madness…like madness.

17.

What else is left but turning to the turns
Of the clock? Changing the soul's desires
Is wrong. Change the sun's.
Darken its bright glow to meet

The soul's. The ill are consumed with illness; they
Have nothing to turn away from. The trees will
Be trees. Fire will always
Burn with fire.

18.

Chained, she walks to her wall & draws an object
that looks like the sun. It's round, with imitative rays

pushed into the cracks of the surface of the cave,
colored by yellow.

The ill are consumed with illness; they have nothing to turn
away from. The trees will always be trees. Fire
will always burn with fire. And why leave the cave
now that you are here with me?

then hot tears fell,
All cries of mourning
he forbade them; sick at heart therefore
In silence

The passage *Don't say mourning. It's too psychoanalytic. I'm not mourning, I'm suffering* is from Roland Barthes's *Mourning Diary.* The line, *I'm going to destroy him*—is adapted from Chekhov's *The Seagulls, I'm going to destroy her because I have nothing better to do.* The final stanza ("then hot tears fell...") is from *the Iliad.*

ANOTHER WORLD OF LIFE

Olena Prygoda

AT THE BEGINNING OF THE WORLD: UKRAINIAN FOLKLORE

Introduction, selection, and translation from Ukrainian by Dr. Nazarii Nazariv

Ukrainian folklore is still a living tradition. Until 1991, anti-Ukrainian authorities in Ukraine did not encourage peasants to pass on authentic singing, but instead imposed artificially created kitsch repertoire. With independence, the elderly, who still remember the authentic manner of singing and the ancient song repertoire, pass on the tradition to the young people who continue to admire this treasure.

What is the value of this treasure in terms of poetry? These are the words with which our ancestors, who did not separate themselves so sharply from nature, directly expressed their emotions. These are songs that were supposed to sound in the landscape, that were themselves the part of the landscape, like a plant or a river. Thence—their great simplicity and strength.

Songs were part of everyday life—they were sung at work, they put children to sleep. Each stage of agricultural work and each stage of life (birth, wedding, death) was accompanied by songs. The songs gave words to express pain and joy. On the basis of mythological motifs, "ballads" appeared, which have nothing to do with the concept of "ballads" in modern poetry. These are the songs with mythological content, which at first could have been a part of weddings and other ceremonies. Spells, charm or 'whispers' were a separate genre that was chanted rather than recited, are short texts that combine pagan and Christian beliefs. They included many ancient mythological images that were to enhance the effectiveness of the word.

Most Ukrainian songs were recorded in the 19th and 20th centuries, although the first recorded Ukrainian folk song dates back to 1571: it was written down by the Czech grammarian Jan Blagoslav. However, the songs were created much earlier. Some motifs are of common Slavic origin. Older documents, in particular ancient chronicles created in Kyiv, contain numerous folklore motifs and entire folklore-based narratives (like the legend about Oleg who died from his horse).

All the texts included in the anthology were translated by me in 2020 in Kyiv and Irpin, which is now beginning to come to life after the brutal occupation by the Russians.

The word heals, the word revives. It is today, when many Ukrainian cities and villages lay wounded and devastated by ruthless enemies, that more than ever it is time for the world to hear and see these amazing texts that have given and continue to give Ukrainians unbreakable strength—strength to be themselves.

PART I. MYTHOLOGICAL BALLADS

1.

Oh, there on the mountain, oh, there on the steep one,
There a couple of grey-blue doves were sitting,
There a couple of grey-blue doves were sitting.

They were sitting, they were mating,
They were hugging with their grey-blue wings,

They were hugging with their grey-blue wings.

Suddenly a hunter, a shooter came,
A hunter, a shooter, a brave lad,
A hunter, a shooter, a brave lad.

He killed a boy-dove, he snatched a girl-dove,
Took her under his skirt, brought her to his home,
Took her under his skirt, brought her to his home.

The girl-dove neither eats nor drinks,
She would fly and cry to the same mountain,
She would fly and cry to the same mountain.

"I've got seven pairs of boy-doves,
Go and choose which will be yours,
Go and choose which will be yours."

He scatterer millet up to her knees,
He poured water up to her wings,
He poured water up to her wings.

"Oh my grey-blue winged dove,
You are so restless,
You are so restless!"

"I was walking, I was looking for,
There is no one like the beloved whom I lost,
There is no one like the beloved whom I lost!"

2.

Oh, I won't go along the bank, I will go across the meadow.
Won't I meet my friend, who is not destined for me?

"Hi, my meadow, my friend, not destined for me!"
"Hi, girl! We used to love each other so much.
We loved each other four years,
We haven't seen each other four weeks,
When we met, we fell ill."

A Cossack is lying in the green grove,
A girl is lying in her mother's larder.

In front of the girl, food and drinks are set;
In front of the cossack, bitter berries are growing.

Cossak is begging his girl: "Give me, my heart, a drink!"

On Sunday morning, all bells are chiming.

"Mom, listen: are they chiming for the cossack?
If for the cossack, dress me up,
Bury me with him in one coffin,
Oh mom, put our heads together,
So that we speak quietly.
Make a high barrow, my mom,
Plant a red guelder rose at our heads.
Erect, mom, golden crosses,
So that people may say: Young lovers are lying here."

3.

In the clear field, there lies a white stone,
On the stone, a grey-blue eagle perched,
The eagle is sitting, the eagle is thinking.

A Cossack is walking a road, he asks the eagle:
"Oh, Eagle, have you been in my land?
Is my beloved one missing me?"

"Oh, she is missing you, she is lying on her bed,
She is holding her right hand at her heart."

Get up, my darling girl, I will tell you the tidings:
Your beloved will come soon, you will have a guest soon!

The beloved got up as if she was waking,
She woke up all the servants:

"Get up, you servants, light up the candles,
Let me look into my lad's eyes!"

"Oh my dear lad, why are you so pale of face?
"Because I haven't seen you so long, my darling"

"Why are you, my dear girl, so pale of face?"
"Because I haven't seen you so long, my darling"

4.

Oh winter-winter, fierce winter!
I beg you, do not freeze me.

Do not freeze me and my husband,
Because even his wife can overcome him.

His wife can overcome him—she doesn't love him any more.

When she loved him—she caressed him,
She took a sharp sword and killed him.
She took a kerchief, brought him to the orchard.
She hanged him amidst the cherry-grove.

Amidst the cherry grove, on a withered oak,
On a withered oak, on a sycamore.

She came back home, she went to the larder,
She poured a bucket and a half of fine wine.
She sat at the table with a strange falcon.
She started drinking wine, she started dropping her tears.

"Oh, woe, woe is to live with such a man!
But it is a bitter woe to live without him.
I will go to the orchard, I will untie him."

At the dawn, she went to her beloved:
"Wake up, my darling, it is already a clear day.
You have hanged enough, you have swayed enough,
You have listened enough to diverse birds,
You have smelled enough wine apples."

5.

In the forest, on the yellow sand,

There is a slim thin tree.
It is slim and thin, its leaf is broad.
Its leaf is broad, its foliage is curly.
On this tree, there sits a grey falcon,
the grey falcon sees far away.
He looks at the clear field, at the blue sea.
In the blue sea, there is a ship afloat.
The ship is afloat, the sea is humming.
Inside the ship, there is a light-filled room.
In the room, there sits a gente lady.
Gentle's lady name is Hannusya.
She sits and she sits, she embroiders three kerchiefs.
The first one she decorates for her father-in-law,
The second one for her mother-in-law,
The third one for her beloved.
I would like to give kerchiefs to them, but who will bring them?
There is no shame, I will bring them myself.
When she entered the yard - a star rose,
She entered the premises as a swallow,
She entered the house as a daughter-in-law.

6.

Ah, in the woods, in the woods, there stood a sycamore.
There stood a sycamore, it was thin and tall.
It was thin, tall, and even curly.
On the sycamore, there sits a nightingale.
The nightingale sits and sings a song.
He would like to go to the blue sea.
On the blue sea, there is a ship afloat.
On that ship, there is a gentle lady,

The gentle lady's name is Hannusya.
She sits, she embroiders a shirt.
Around the neck, she puts diverse birds.
On the sleeves, she puts grey doves.

7.
Oh, a warrior came from Ukraine,
He snatched a girl from her family,
He snatched a girl from her family.

"Oh, girl, come with us,
You will live better, than at your mom's,
You will live better, than at your mom's.

At your mom's, you wore a patched shirt,
At us, you will wear red clothes,
At us, you will wear red clothes."

Oh, stupid girl, stupid one, she believed him,
She mounted a horse, she rode away with the warrior,
She mounted a horse, she rode away with the warrior.

He rode her to the dark wood:
"Take off, girl, the wreath from your head,
Take off the wreath from your head."

Oh, the girl cries, the girl cries and faints,
She takes off the wreath—the wreath from her head,
She takes off the wreath—the wreath from her head.

He rode the girl among the yellow sands:
"Take off, girl, the ribbons from your head,
Take off, girl, the ribbons from your head".

Oh, the girl cries, the girl cries and faints,
She takes off the ribbons—the ribbons from her head,
She takes off the ribbons—the ribbons from her head.

He took took her by her sides,
He hurled her into the deep Dunay,
He hurled her into the deep Dunay.

Oh, the girl cries, the girl cries and faints,
She clings to the bank with her hands,
She clings to the bank with her hands.

Oh, a cossack took out his sable,
He cut her arms up to the elbow,
He cut her arms up to the elbow.

Her brother saw it from the high rampart,
He descended to her by a silken cord,
He descended to her by a silken cord:

"Oh, sister, it seems you hadn't enough luxury,
So you became a rascal's help,
So you became a rascal's help."

"Oh, I had enough luxury,
But I didn't know that there is woe,

But I didn't know that there is woe."

8.

Across the Dunay,
Across the Dunay,
There a shepherd grazes sheep.

He grazes them, he grazes,
He grazes them, he grazes,
He shouts to the young lads:

"Oh you lads, brave lads,
Oh you lads, brave lads,
Tell my girl,

"She shouldn't wait for me,
She shouldn't wait for me,
She should marry someone else!"

As soon as the girl heard this,
She hurried home:
"My dear mother!

"What should I do?
What should I do?
Boys are not willing to love me!"

"Go, my daughter, to the grove,
Go, my daughter, to the grove,
Dig up herbs and roots."

“I don’t know the herbs,
I don’t know the herbs,
I will ask people about them.”

She dug up roots,
She dug up roots,
From under the white stone,

Washed it in the river,
Washed it in the river,
Boiled in milk.

The root hadn’t boiled enough,
The root hadn’t boiled enough,
When shepherd came flying.

“Oh, what brought you here,
Oh, what brought you here,
A boat or an oar?’

“A grey horse brought me,
A grey horse brought me
To the girl’s courtyard.”

9.
“There are two of us, two of us,
We are two friends.
Come out, a girl,
You will be the third one.”

"How can I
come out to you,
You are two, I am alone,
You will make me freeze."

"Don't be afraid, oh girl,
Don't be afraid of frost,
I will put your white feet
Into my winter hat."

"Your hat
is too good for this,
I am just a girl,
A young girl!"

It was not a girl who came out,
It was her mother:
"Welcome, o son-in-law,
Welcome to my cabin."

No sooner I stepped
into the room from the porch,
They gave me
a chair to sit.

No sooner I sit
On the chair,
They gave me
A quail to eat.

I ate only
A wing, a rib,
And something stuck
In my chest, at my heart.

A young girl
Laughs through the window,
Because a young lad
Is swaying in his saddle.

"Don't laugh, oh girl,
For God's sake, don't laugh!
I was treated by you
With poison.

"Go bring here
My old mom,
She will conjure
This sheer poison."

"Your old mom
Won't be helpful,
The only thing will be -
A new coffin."

10.

There flows a deep Dunay,
There stands a high hall,
There stands a high hall.

From the hall's door,
A young widow came forth,
A young widow came forth.

A young widow came forth,
She gave birth to her two sons,
She gave birth to her two sons.

She wrapped them in silk,
She let them flow in Dunay,
She let them flow in Dunay.

"Oh you, quiet Dunay,
Do not harm my children,
Do not harm my children.

"Oh you, cold water,
Take care of my two sons,
Take care of my two sons."

Twenty years went past,
The widow went to fetch water,
The widow went to fetch water.

She was scooping water,
A ship came floating,
A ship came floating.
Aboard the ship,
There were two young lads from Don,
There were two young lads from Don.

One of them takes off his hat,
He asks the widow,
He asks the widow:

"Oh you, young widow,
Will you marry a young lad from Don?
Will you marry a young lad from Don?"

"I will marry a lad from Don,
I will marry my daughter to another,
I will marry my daughter to another."

The night passes by,
A brother asks his sister,
A brother asks his sister:

"Tell me the truth,
Of what family are you,
Of what family are you?"

"My father's name is Karpo,
My name is Olena,
My name is Olena."

"My name is Vasyl,
My father's name is Karpo,
My father's name is Karpo".

"Let the mother perish,
She married a sister to a brother,

She married a sister to a brother!

"Let's go, my brother, to the dark forest,
Let a beast devour us,
Let a beat devour us!"

"Let's go, my sister, across the field,
Let's cast upon the soil like herbs,
Let's cast upon the soil like herbs.

"You will give a blue blossom,
I will give a yellow blossom,
So that all the world knows!"

11.

In the meadows, there is a willow
That grows without a root.

In the village, there is a widow
that lived seven years without her husband.

She lived seven years without her husband,
She loved two young merchants.

She loved two young merchants,
She gave birth to two sons.

She gave birth to two sons,
Ivanyusha and Vasyl.

She wrapt them in silk,
She wrapt them in silk,
She brought them to Dunay.

"Oh, you river Dunay,
Take care of my children.

"Oh, you, thick reads,
Cook dinner for my children!

"And you, yellow sand,
Feed my children!"

After eighteen years,
Widow came to fetch water.

The widow bent to scoop water,
A ship approached her.
A ship approached her,
A seaman looked at her.

The seamen looked at her,
He started asking her:

"Oh you, widow, oh widow,
Would you marry me?"
"I would marry you,
I would marry my daughter to another!"

PART II. RITUAL SONGS

1.

At the beginning of the world, there was nothing,
Blow, God, blow with sacred spirit over the earth
Neither sky nor earth,
Blow, God, blow with sacred spirit over the earth
Only a blue sea was everywhere,
Blow, God, blow with sacred spirit over the earth
In the middle of the sea, there stood a green sycamore.
Blow, God, blow with sacred spirit over the earth
On the sycamore, three doves sat,
Blow, God, blow with sacred spirit over the earth
Three doves held a council,
Blow, God, blow with sacred spirit over the earth
They discussed how to lay foundations of the world.
Blow, God, blow with sacred spirit over the earth
"Let us dive to the bottom of the sea,
Blow, God, blow with sacred spirit over the earth
Let us get fine sand,
Blow, God, blow with sacred spirit over the earth
Let us sow the fine sand,
Blow, God, blow with sacred spirit over the earth
It will form the black earth for us.
Blow, God, blow with sacred spirit over the earth
Let us take a golden stone,
Blow, God, blow with sacred spirit over the earth
Let us sow the golden stone,
Blow, God, blow with sacred spirit over the earth
It will form the clear sky for us,

Blow, God, blow with sacred spirit over the earth
The clear sky, the shiny sun,
Blow, God, blow with sacred spirit over the earth
The shiny sun, the clear moon,
Blow, God, blow with sacred spirit over the earth
The clear moon, the clear morning star,
Blow, God, blow with sacred spirit over the earth
The clear morning star, the fine stars."
Blow, God, blow with sacred spirit over the earth

2.
The moon met the fine rain,
Glorified art thou, our dear God in the sky!
And the rain says: "Nobody's greater than me!
Glorified art thou, our dear God in the sky!
I will sprinkle rye and grain,
Glorified art thou, our dear God in the sky!
Rye and grain, all the seeds, all the spring crops.
Glorified art thou, our dear God in the sky!
And the moon says: "Nobody's greater than me!
Glorified art thou, our dear God in the sky!
I will illumine mountains and valleys,
Glorified art thou, our dear God in the sky!
Mountains and valleys, the sacred earth,
Glorified art thou, our dear God in the sky!
The sacred earth, and all good people."
Glorified art thou, our dear God in the sky!

3.
Oh, wind blew from above and from beneath,

River Dunay was dry and overgrown by green herbs.
It was overgrown by willow, by different flowers.
A wondrous animal rescues the green herbs,
The green herbs are rescued by a grey deer.
The deer has fifty horns,
Fifty horns and one plate on them.
On that plate, there is a golden chair,
On the golden chair, a gentle lad sits,
He plays a harp, he sings nice songs.

4.
Oh, in the orchard, peacocks are strolling.
Peacocks are strolling and letting their feathers fall.

A comely lady strolls after them,
She picks the feathers, she puts them in her sleeve.
She takes them from her sleeve, she puts them on the table.
She takes them from the table, she waves a wreath.

She tries the wreath on her head:
"Mother, look if it befits me well"

Early-early in the morning, the girl went to fetch water.
Oh, tempestuous winds came together,
tempestuous winds and heavy rains,
They threw the wreath under the lofty bank,
Under the lofty bank, into the deep Dunay.

The wreath floats along the Dunay,
The girl follows it ashore.

She meets three fishermen,
Three fishermen are a great lord's servants.
"God bless you, God bless you, three fishermen,
Three fishermen, the great lord's servants!
Haven't you met, haven't you picked
Peacock's wreath made of periwinkle?"
"Yes, we met it, yes, we picked it,
But what will you give us for it?"
The first one will get a golden ring,
The second will get a kerchief from her waist,
The third one will get the girl herself,
The young girl is like a berry.

5.
A father had a new hall,
A garden grew around it.

A gilded garden grew around,
There was a green vine in the garden.

The vine was guarded by a young girl,
She guarded and sewed her sewing,
She sewed her sewing and fell fast asleep.

Lo, birds of paradise came flying,
They sat down, they fell on the gilded dew.

The gilded dew tinkled,
The girl awoke from her slumbers:

"Shoo, shoo, the birds of paradise!
My father didn't planted the garden for you,
Planted garden and bedewed it with gold.
I myself need the green vine:
My brother is going to marry,
I am also going to become a bride."

PART III. SPELLS AND CHARMS

1.
Oh Moon-Prince! There are three of you:
the first in the sky,
the second on the earth,
the third in the sea - a white stone.
As they cannot come together,
let my toothache cease!

2.
There is the Moon in the sky,
there is a corpse in the grave,
there is a stone in the sea:
when these three brothers
come together
to hold a feast,
let my teeth hurt.

3.
O Moon, oh young Prince!
Have you visited the old Moon?

Have you asked him if he had a
toothache?
Let my teeth never hurt, in ages and
judgements.
There is a hare in the fields,
there is a fish in the sea,
there is the Moon in the sky:
when these three brothers feast together,
let my teeth ache.

4.

From wherever you came,
From wherever you crept,
I chase you out,
I conjure you out,
I curse you,
Go away,
Go to the woods,
Go to the reeds,
Go to the meadows,
Go to the passages,
Creep inside an asp,
Creep inside a toad!
Away, away!

5.

In the morning of St George's day let you gather sky's dew
into a napkin till it is wet, and take it to your home,
and press this dew into a glass.

If any cattle happens to have a wall-eye,
utter the following, standing in front of it:

St George rode a white horse
with white lips,
with white teeth,
he was white himself,
he was clad in white,
his belt was white,
he leads three hounds:
the first one is white,
the second one is grey,
the third one is red.
The white one will lick a wall-eye away,
the grey one—a tear,
the red one—blood.

6.

There on the mountain,
oxen ploughed the soil
and sowed red mallow;
the red mallow didn't sprout.
There stood a girl.
On the shore of the blue sea,
there stood a ribless sheep.
On the shore of the red sea,
there lies a red stone.
Where the Sun walks,
there blood stops.

Where the Sun sets,
there blood dries.

7.
A red man walked,
he was carrying a bucket of water,
the man stumbled,
the bucket broke,
water spilled,
the grey horse stopped bleeding.

8.
Three rivers flew
under the viburnum leaf:
the first one of water,
the second one of milk,
the third one of blood.
A watery one I will drink,
a milky one I will eat,
a bloody one I will quench,
I will stop bleeding
of the grey horse.

9.
A black raven flew
from the steep rock,
perched on the grey horse's rump,
from its rump to its back,
from its back to its mane,
from its mane to the ground.

10.

Three brothers walked,
they talked, they asked a rabid dog:
"Go the right way
across the Jordan river,
ascend the high mountain,
there is a ram rambling
with huge horns,
shave his wool
between the horns,
and come back:
scoop up water from Jordan,
slash a white stone from the rock.
Let all saint Guardians help me
to conjure, to incantate
the rabid dog!

11.

In the field-field,
In the steppe-steppe,
there is a pear tree,
under the tree, there is a golden bed,
on this bed, there is a snake.
"I came to you, oh snake,
to ask you and god to have mercy on me:
a harm happened to my bay horse
(or a mare, or an ox, or a cow)
of yellow bones, of black blood,
of red meat, of raven wool.
Summon your kings, your generals,

your princes, hetmans,
colonels, centurions,
thains, chiefs, bannermen,
soldiers-cossacks,
all officers from homes,
from earth,
from dung,
from grass,
from stone,
from water,
from cellars,
from under the heaps,
and make them to beat
the guilty with an oak club,
make him sink in humid soil,
in yellow sand
for thirty sajen deep!

12.
In the sea, in the ocean,
on the Buyan island,
there stood a hollow oak,
under that oak,
there sat a turtle,
the chief of all the vipers.
Snake, snake, teach well your nephews,
else I'll find such a man that devours
Wednesdays and Fridays,
and he will devour you!

13.

—Good evening for you, Fire Dragon!
—Hello, girl, begotten one, baptized one, prayed for!
—Where are you flying?
—I am flying to burn the woods, to dry the soil,
to make grass wither.
—Do not fly, oh Fire Dragon,
to burn the woods,
to dry the soil,
to make grass wither!
But fly to the cossack's courtyard,
and wherever you catch him—
amidst the meadows,
on his way,
at his meal,
in his bed—
grip his heart,
make him languish,
make him burn!
Make him quiver and tremble
after me, begotten one,
baptized, and prayed for!
Let him not eat me out,
let him not drink me out,
let him not forget me
while playing with others,
let me always be in his mind.
Drag him—cossack Ivan,
the begotten one,

baptized, and prayed for—
to me,
whose name is Maria-maiden,
the begotten one, baptized, and prayed for!

14.
There has been a hollow man,
who had hollow oxen,
a hollow plough,
and hollow ploughboys.
They ploughed a hollow field,
he sowed hollow grain.
Hollow grain has sprouted,
has ripened,
hollow reapers harvested it
with a hollow sickle,
put it in hollow sacks,
brought it to a hollow city,
milled it on a hollow stone,
scattered erysipelas
among huts, among marshes,
among hollow reeds.

15.
If you are a depressing fever,
if you are a shaking fever,
if you are from waters,
if you are from winds,
if you are from whirlwind,
if you are from thoughts,

if you are sent forth,
if you are from sleep,
if you are from food,
if you are from a drink,
if you are from the land,
if you are from chanting,
if you are from conjuring,
if you are sent forth,
if you are of an hour,
if you are of half an hour,
if you are of a day or a midday,
if you are of a night or midnight,
you were steady, you were thriving,
till I didn't know you.
Now when I know you,
I am sending you forth from the bones,
I will pour water on your face,
I will burn your eyes,
I will conjure you with prayers,
I will send away from Christian faith:
Go away, where dogs are not barking,
where rooster doesn't sing,
where Christian voice doesn't go.

16.

Under the sun, under the hot one,
under the wood, under the dark one,
there stands a willow.
Under this willow,
there are seven hundred roots,

on this willow,
there are seven hundred cords.
On these cords, there sits Khan King
and Khan Queen.

17.

On the Ossiyan mountain,
there stood a stone well.
A stone girl went there,
stone buckets and stone yoke,
stone braid,
and she was of stone.
If she fetches water from there,
let the begotten, baptized God's servant Ivan bleed again.

18.

Oak, oak!
You are black,
you have a white birch,
you have small oaks—your sons,
you have small birches—your daughters.
Let you, oak and birch,
whisper and hum,
let God's servant Ivan,
the begotten one,
baptized, sleep and grow!

19.

In the Diyan sea,
on the Kiyan island,

there stood an oak,
in the oak, there was a hole,
in the hole, there was a nest,
in the nest, there were three Queens:
the first was Kiliyana,
the second Iliyana,
the third Spindle-Queen.
You, Spindle-Queen,
come forth, whistle to your army—
army from the fields,
from the woods, from the waters,
from dung, from home!
Prohibit it, oh Spindle-Queen,
to bite where it shouldn't,
to use their teeth—
because their teeth will be no more,
they will fall down on the ground
from a begotten one,
baptized one
God's servant Ivan.

20.

There is the Moon in the sky,
an oak in the wood,
a pike in the sea,
a bear in the forest,
a beast in the field.
When they come together
to have a feast,
let N's teeth ache.

21.

An eagle flew across the sea,
lowered its wing,
quenched the spring.
A rooster perched on a stone
and waves with its wings.
The stone doesn't move,
the Christian blood
of the begotten one, baptized,
prayed for
Ivan
doesn't flow.

22.

A girl walked an evil route,
she went to an evil orchard
to pluck evil herbs,
to cut it with an evil knife,
to brew an evil stew,
the stew starts to boil,
blood ceases to flow.

23.

Immaculate Virgin
walked along the blue sea,
she leaned on the golden stick.
She encountered St Peter.
"Where are you going, Immaculate one?"
"Towards the place,
where three brothers fought,

to enchant their blood."
The wound closed,
the blood stopped,
the Immaculate one came back.
Amen!

24.

A mountain is with a mountain,
a stone is with grass,
a fish is with water!
When they come together,
when the stone flows,
when water stands still,
let then the teeth
of the begotten one, pried for,
baptized N ache.

25.

At the seaside, there is a green withe.
Wind withers the green withe,
wind withers it, blows away its leaves.
One leaf fell into the sea,
another fell into the heart,
the third one will heal the wound,
will cure the wound!

26.

Before whispering, let you splash some water on the child,
and then you shall say:

Oh stars, stars!
You are three sisters in the sky:
the first one at sunset,
the second at midnight,
the third at the dawn.
Be helpful for me in some sickness.
Pervade meadows and banks,
roots and stones,
pervade also this begotten one,
baptized N!

SQUIRREL

Tatyana Shramko

ONLY I KNOW

Tatyana Shramko

PATCHING CLOUDS

Olga Nadukhovskaya

BIOGRAPHIES

ODARKA BILOKON *is a writer and translator based in Kyiv, Ukraine. She is a graduate of the Philology Master's Degree Program at Kyiv National Linguistic University. Her works have appeared in several Ukrainian anthologies and* 3:AM Magazine.

MARIA DZIEDZAN *was born in Lincolnshire, England to a Welsh mother and a Ukrainian father, who had come to the UK as a POW in 1947. She was brought up to love a country she did not see until after Ukraine's independence in 1991 when she visited Kyiv and then her father's village, Snovydiv, in Western Ukraine. This visit inspired her to retire from teaching English in Nottinghamshire and to write her trilogy of novels, My Lost Country, about the terrors experienced by her fellow countrymen and women during the Second World War. The first of these novels, When Sorrows Come, is available on Amazon.*

VICTORIA FESHCHUK *is a poet, translator, and special projects editor at Chytomo, Ukrainian media of literature and book publishing. She is also the Co-founder of the Serpen—a platform for Polish poetry translation. She graduated from the National University of Taras Shevchenko in Kyiv in the department of literary analysis. She also studied at the Jagiellonian University*

(Kraków, Poland) as a part of a scholarship program for Young Scientists from the East. She has been a laureate of national poetry competitions and has participated at several Ukrainian literary festivals. She lives in Kyiv.

STELLA HAYES *is the author of the poetry collection* One Strange Country *(What Books Press, 2020). She grew up in Brovary, a suburb outside of Kyiv, Ukraine, and in Los Angeles, California. She earned a creative writing degree at University of Southern California and is currently a graduate student at NYU, studying for an M.F.A in poetry. Her work has been nominated for the Best of the Net and the Pushcart Prize and has appeared in Poetry Project's The Recluse, The Lake, Prelude, Spillway, and is forthcoming from Stanford's Mantis, and Poet Lore, among others. She is the assistant fiction editor, as well as the online features editor, of* Dispatches from Ukraine *at Washington Square Review.*

NICK HERRING *is a 35-year-old English teacher from Kyiv, where he remains to this day and intends to stay no matter what the future holds. After sending his family to another country for safety, he decided to write about the war in Ukraine.*

IRYNA IVANKOVYCH *is a translator, linguist, literary critic, and editor currently residing in Pennsylvania. Born in Ukraine, she received her Master's Degree at the University of Warsaw Institute of Applied Linguistics. She became a Doctor of Philosophy at the Ukrainian Free University in the field of sociolinguistics in 2012. She is the president of the St. Sophia Religious Association of Ukrainian Catholics and the director of the Josyf Slipyj Research Center. She is the founder and director of the*

ESL.Ukraine charity platform.

RIMMA KRANET *is a Ukrainian-American writer with a Bachelor's Degree in English from University of California Los Angeles. Her work has appeared in* Brilliant Flash Fiction, Construction Lit, Coal Hill Review, EcoTheo Collective, The Common Breath, Drunk Monkey, Door Is A Jar Magazine *and in* The Short Vigorous Roots: A Contemporary Flash Fiction Collection of Migrant Voices. *She resides between Florence, Italy and Los Angeles, California.*

SOFIIA KRAZHAN *is a Ukrainian first-year university student at NYU. Raised in Kyiv, she moved between countries in Eastern Europe before graduating high school in Finland and moving to the States to pursue an International Relations major, later hoping to earn a J.D & Ph.D in International Law.*

HALYNA KRUK *(Lviv, Ukraine, 1974) is a writer, translator, and literary critic. She holds a Ph.D. in Ukrainian Literature and is currently researching Ukrainian medieval literature. She is the author of five poetry books—*Journeys in Search of a Home, Footprints on Sand *(both 1997),* The Face beyond the Photograph *(2005),* Co(an)existence *(2013),* An Adult Woman *(2017), and a collection of short stories* Anyone but Me *(2021). Her poems and short stories were translated into more than 20 languages. She is a member of the Ukrainian PEN and a professor of literary studies at Lviv National University.*

R.B. LEMBERG *is a poet, fantasist, and professor living in Lawrence, Kansas. R.B.'s LGBTQIA-themed books were shortlisted for the*

Nebula, Locus, World Fantasy, Crawford, and other awards. R.B. was born in L'viv, Ukraine. Follow them on Twitter at @rb_lemberg

LARYSA MARTYNIUK *is a visual artist residing in Colorado, USA, who works in oil, acrylic, watercolor and mixed media. The world of nature provides myriads of beautiful forms and colors to which the artist turns for inspiration. Being first generation Ukrainian American born to Ukrainian parents, the unprovoked war raging in Ukraine has underscored her love for her ancestral land. "Storm Clouds over Ukraine" depicts the horror of missiles striking Ukraine and the fear of losing not only Larysa's people but the beautiful cultural centers and decades old architecture.*

OLGA NADUKHOVSKAYA *is a San Francisco-based artist working in acrylic on canvas. She had no professional art training, which gave her the encouragement and freedom to create using her imagination instead of trying to balance between educational training and personal expressions. She was born in Kyiv, the capital of Ukraine. She lived there for half of her life, surrounded by kind, warm and generous people who want to see the bright sun shining in the blue sky above Ukraine. Olga was surrounded by beautiful nature, colorful folk costumes, and rich cultural traditions, all of which she reflects in her paintings. You can find her online at www.makasha.me*

NAZARII NAZARIV, *PhD, was born in 1990 in a small village in Ukrainian Steppe, a protected nature preserve. Now he lives in Kyiv, Ukraine, where he works as a translator, a linguist, and a researcher. He writes his poems in Ukrainian and English. His Ukrainian poems were selected for representative national* *anthologies, whereas his English poems and translations have appeared in* Eratio, Eunoia, Literary Shanghai, *and* The Tiger Moth Review.

OLENA PRYGODA *was born in 1985 in the village of Klavdiyevo, Kyiv region, Borodyanka district. As a second-year student at Poltava Pedagogical University, she worked as an editor of artistic and journalistic programs for Poltava Regional Radio. In 2017, she won the All-Ukrainian competition for the development of original drawings of postage stamps. Olena has been living in Murcia, Spain since 2018.*

LEX SHRAMKO *is currently working on a World War II fairytale braided from memoir and biography, set in both the past and present, about her mother, a Ukrainian war orphan who discovers her existence as an 85 year-old-woman. Recent publications include* Moonpark Review, Gargoyle, *and* Broadkill Review. *She resides in Alexandria, Virginia.*

TATYANA SHRAMKO *was born in Harbin, China, and lived in Kharkiv, Ukraine during WW2 before fleeing in 1943. She now resides in Alexandria, Virginia, where she has a studio at the Torpedo Art Factory. http://www.shramkodesign.com/*

ASKOLD SKALSKY *was born in Chernivtsi, Ukraine. He came to the United States at the end of World War II, fleeing with his family before the Red Army when it occupied the Bukovina province. He is now a retired college professor living in Frederick, Maryland. His poems have appeared in numerous magazines and online journals in the USA as well as in Europe, Canada, and Asia.*

SOFIIA TIAPKINA *is a sophomore at Northfield Mount Hermon School in Gill, Massachusetts. She is a passionate writer and an aspiring visual artist. A native of Kryvyi Rih in southern Ukraine, Sofiia constantly worries about her family, who remain in Ukraine. She organizes informational and fundraising events at her school and works with Ukraine Global Scholars to support Ukraine.*

KATERYNA VOLOSHYNA *is an author from Ukraine. She lives in Dnipro City. She has a Master's Degree in History and Philosophy. Kateryna is fascinated by legends, fairy tales with a twist, and mysterious stories. She works as a content writer.*

ELLA YEVTUSHENKO *is a Ukrainian poet, translator and musician from Kyiv. Finalist of several poetry contests in Ukraine, participant of book festivals such as Book Arsenal, Ї, BookForum, Translatorium etc. Her first poetry book* Lichtung *was published in 2016. Her poems have been translated to ten languages. In 2020 she founded a solo electronic & poetic project Thuyone. Due to the Russian aggression in Ukraine, she had to temporarily move to Lviv, but hopes to return to her native Kyiv soon.*

GLOSSARY OF UKRAINIAN TERMS

Belarus. A small European country that borders both Ukraine and Russia.
Boje upasi. "God forbid."
Borsch. A red beet soup and Ukraine's national dish.
Brovory. A suburb of Kyiv in northern Ukraine.
Chechnya. The site of centuries-long armed conflict between independence and Russian annexation. Russia controls the region, now called the Chechen Republic, as of 2017.
Chernihiv. A city in northern Ukraine.
Chornobaivka. A city in the Kherson region of Ukraine. Russian forces attempted to take control of the city in February 2022 because of its airport, which could have acted as a gateway for Russians to control major Ukrainian cities. As of April 17, 2022, Ukrainian forces control the city.
Cossack. One of a semi-nomadic, self-ruled community of East Slavic. Orthodox Christian horsemen who originated in Ukrainian and Russian steppes in the 14th century.
Crimea. A southern region of Ukraine until March 2014, when Russia invaded and annexed it.
Dnieper River. The fourth-longest river in Europe and the longest river in Ukraine, cutting through Russia, Belarus, and central Ukraine. Also spelled 'Dnipro.'
Donbas. A historically, culturally, and economically prominent region in southeastern Ukraine.
Emsk Decree. A secret decree of the Russian Empire in 1876 in which the Ukrainian language was banned in print, with the sole exception of reprinting old documents.
Horlivka. A city in the Donbas region of Ukraine known for its source of coal.
Irpin. A Ukrainian city located next to Kyiv.
Kadyrov. Refers to Ramzan Kadyrov, the Russian president of the Chechen Republic (formerly Chechnya).

Kalyna. "Highbush cranberry" or Guelder Rose, a symbol of Ukraine, its freedom, love, and loyalty.
Kharkiv. A city in northeast Ukraine. The capital city of the Ukrainian Soviet Socialist Republic until 1934, when Kyiv became Ukraine's capital.
Kherson. A city in southern Ukraine.
Kyiv. Capital city of Ukraine.
Lviv. The largest city in western Ukraine and the sixth-largest Ukrainian city overall. It is close to the Ukrainian-Polish border. The city is known for its coffee, churches, and lion statues.
Mariupol. The tenth-largest city in Ukraine, situated in the southeast.
Mavka. A long-haired, female spirit in Ukrainian mythology who represents the souls of girls who have died tragic, unnatural, or premature deaths. They are often dangerous to young men.
Oskolki. Detritus or debris.
Paska. A Ukrainian bread made for the Easter holiday.
Perestroika. "Restructuring" in Russian. Refers to the economic and political restructuring of the Soviet Union in the 1980s by Mikhail Gorbachev and the Communist Party.
Razkol. A schism or split.
Rinok. The central market square of Lviv, Ukraine.
Rosynka. Little dewdrop.
Samizdat. The reproduction of censored literature into makeshift. publications, often handmade and distributed secretly across Eastern Europe.
Sajen. A unit of measurement. 1 sajen equals about 2 meters.
Semeinoe delo. "Family business."
Solzhenitsyn. Refers to Aleksandr Solzhenitsyn, a Russian novelist and Soviet dissident known for his help raising global awareness of the crimes against humanity of the Soviet regime in the 20th century.
Sopilka. A variety of flute-like instruments used by Ukrainian folk musicians. Most commonly refers to a fife with six to ten finger holes.
Steppe: Flat grassland with no foliage in Eastern Europe.
Ternopil: A city in western Ukraine, on the River Dnieper, known for its system of caves.
Україна понад усе. Ukraina ponad use. "Ukraine above all."
Ullmar (Old English). A name meaning "fame of the wolf."
Valuyev Decree. A secret decree of the Russian Empire in 1863 in which Ukrainian language publications were forbidden.
Velukden. "Great Day."
Zelensky. Refers to Volodymyr Zelensky, the president of Ukraine.

Printed in Great Britain
by Amazon